HIKIKOMORI: UNDERSTANDING AND OVERCOMING SOCIAL ISOLATION

Mark Spencer

ISBN:9798878882941

DEDICATION

This book is dedicated to all individuals navigating the challenging journey of Hikikomori. May it serve as a beacon of hope and understanding, illuminating the path towards healing and recovery. Your resilience and strength inspire us, and it is our sincere hope that this book brings comfort and guidance during difficult times. You are not alone, and together, we can overcome the shadows of social withdrawal. Let this book be a source of solace and empowerment as you embark on your journey towards a brighter tomorrow.

With heartfelt wishes,

Mark Spencer

CONTENTS

ACKNOWLEDGMENTS

I extend my heartfelt gratitude to the Department of Applied Psychology, Zurich, for their invaluable support and guidance throughout the creation of this book on Hikikomori. Special thanks are owed to Simone Amendola for their insightful commentary and contributions to the field, which have enriched our understanding of social withdrawal and its complexities. Furthermore, we extend our appreciation to all individuals who have contributed their expertise, shared their experiences, and supported our endeavor to shed light on Hikikomori.

HIKIKOMORI
Understanding and Overcoming Social Isolation
Accredited and reliable work by
MARK SPENCER

CHAPTER 1: INTRODUCTION TO HIKIKOMORI AND UNDERSTANDING SOCIAL ISOLATION

Social isolation is a universal aspect of the human experience, often resulting from a variety of factors such as personal choice, mental health issues, or societal pressures. While it is normal for individuals to crave occasional solitude, some find themselves engulfed in a state of extreme withdrawal from social interactions, leading to a condition known as Hikikomori. In this chapter, we explore the fundamental aspects of Hikikomori, shed light on its prevalence, and delve into the detrimental consequences it can have on individuals and society. Hikikomori, a term originating from Japan, refers to a phenomenon wherein individuals retreat from social life and isolate themselves within their homes for an extended period, typically six months or more. These individuals often rely on their families to meet their basic needs, leading to a heavy burden on both the individuals and their loved ones. While Hikikomori appears more common in Japan due to cultural and societal factors, reports suggest that similar cases exist worldwide, indicating that this is not just a Japanese issue.

It is important to note that Hikikomori is not a formally recognized mental health disorder in the Diagnostic and Statistical Manual of Mental Disorders (DSM-5). However, it is crucial to acknowledge its impact on those who experience it and the wider society. Reports estimate that there are millions of Hikikomori individuals globally, although obtaining accurate prevalence rates is challenging due to underreporting and the hidden nature of this condition.

Studies

Understanding the experiences of hikikomori through the lens of the CHIME framework: This study was conducted by Jolene Y. K. Yung, Victor Wong, Grace W. K. Ho & Alex Molassiotis and published in BMC Psychology on July 10, 20211.

Identifying Social Withdrawal (Hikikomori) Factors in Adolescents: This study was conducted by Yukiko Hamasaki, Nancy Pionnié-Dax, Géraldine Dorard, Nicolas Tajan & Takatoshi Hikida and published in Child Psychiatry & Human Development on September 21, 2020.

Finding the biological roots for pathological social withdrawal, Hikikomori: This study was conducted by researchers at Kyushu University and published on June 1, 2022.

Insights from Hikikomori (prolonged social withdrawal) for global psychiatry: This study was conducted by Dr. Marcus P.J. Tan and published in BJPsych International on May 17, 2021.

Chaos and confusion in Hikikomori research: This commentary was written by Simone Amendola from the Department of Applied Psychology, Zurich University of Applied Sciences, Zurich, Switzerland and published in Frontiers in Psychiatry on May 17, 2023.

Contributing factors

The factors contributing to Hikikomori are multifaceted, making it difficult to pinpoint a single cause. Sociocultural and economic pressures, academic stress, bullying, family dysfunction, and mental health issues have all been identified as potential triggers. Individuals affected by Hikikomori often struggle with low self-esteem, anxiety, depression, and other mental health conditions. In turn, these factors, combined with the perpetuating cycle of isolation, can intensify the social withdrawal and create a self-reinforcing pattern.

The consequences of Hikikomori are profound, affecting not only the individuals themselves but also their families and society as a whole. For individuals, prolonged isolation can exacerbate pre-existing mental health conditions, hinder personal growth, and limit opportunities for social and emotional development. As a result, Hikikomori individuals often face difficulties in obtaining employment, maintaining relationships, or reintegrating into society once they decide to seek help.

Family members of Hikikomori individuals bear a heavy emotional and financial burden. They experience stress, guilt, and helplessness, as they struggle to understand and support their loved ones who are trapped in this state of isolation. The lack of awareness and societal stigma surrounding Hikikomori further compounds the challenges faced by both individuals and their families.

As a consequence, family relationships may become strained, and the ripple effects can extend to wider social networks, perpetuating a cycle of isolation and despair.

Moreover, the social and economic impact of Hikikomori should not be overlooked. A study conducted by the National Institute of Mental Health in Japan estimated that Hikikomori-related costs, including healthcare and lost productivity, amounted to billions of dollars annually. Such staggering figures highlight the urgency of addressing this issue and developing effective strategies to tackle social isolation.

Understanding the complexity of Hikikomori and its implications is the first step towards finding viable solutions and support systems for individuals affected. By raising awareness, debunking misconceptions, and fostering empathy, we can contribute to a more compassionate society that promotes inclusivity and mental well-being. The second half of this chapter will delve deeper into the underlying factors contributing to Hikikomori, exploring potential interventions and strategies to overcome the challenges faced by those affected.

Now we will delve deeper into the underlying factors contributing to Hikikomori, exploring potential interventions and strategies to overcome the challenges faced by those affected.

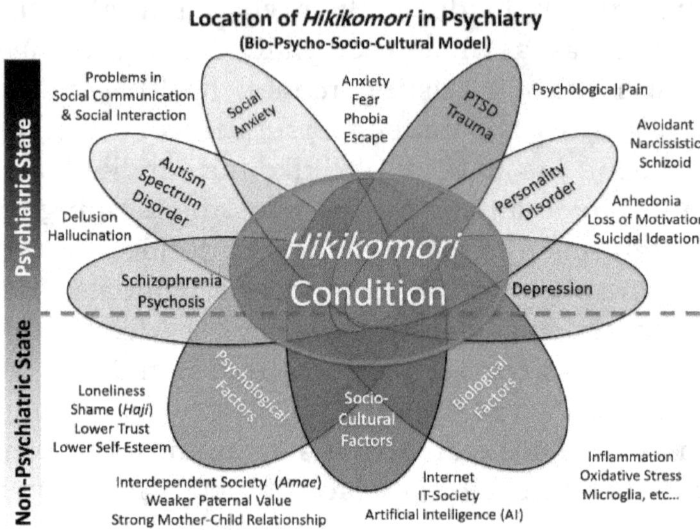

Understanding the complex web of factors that contribute to Hikikomori is crucial in order to develop effective interventions. Numerous studies have identified sociocultural and economic pressures as significant triggers for Hikikomori. In Japan, where Hikikomori is most commonly associated, the cultural emphasis placed on conformity, achievement, and success can lead to immense academic pressure. The intense competition and rigid expectations of educational institutions, coupled with a fear of failure, can drive individuals to retreat from social life as they strive to meet perceived societal expectations. Similarly, the stigmatization of mental health issues in many cultures can lead individuals to withdraw out of shame or fear of judgment.

Bullying and family dysfunction also play a role in the development of Hikikomori. For some individuals, negative experiences in school or community settings can foster a deep sense of isolation and mistrust, leading to a withdrawal from social interactions. Additionally, dysfunctional family dynamics, such as high levels of conflict or emotional neglect, can contribute to feelings of alienation and the desire to escape from social interactions.

Mental health issues are prevalent among individuals affected by Hikikomori, often acting as both the cause and consequence of social isolation. Conditions such as depression, anxiety disorders, and social anxiety disorder can heighten the individual's perception of the world as a threatening and unwelcoming place, leading to further withdrawal. Moreover, the lack of social support and social skills resulting from prolonged isolation can perpetuate and intensify existing mental health challenges.

Addressing Hikikomori requires a multi-faceted approach considering the interconnected nature of its underlying factors. The first step in intervention is to raise awareness and reduce the societal stigma surrounding Hikikomori. Educating the public, including teachers, healthcare providers, and families, about the condition can promote understanding and empathy. This knowledge will assist in identifying individuals at risk, offering support, and reducing the isolation they experience.

Early intervention is crucial in preventing the escalation of Hikikomori. Identifying and addressing the triggers and risk factors in individuals' lives, such as academic stress or family conflicts, can help alleviate the pressure and prevent social withdrawal. Providing counseling and therapy services, both individual and family-based, can equip individuals with coping mechanisms and improve their emotional well-being. Group therapy sessions, where individuals can connect with peers experiencing similar challenges, can also be beneficial in fostering a sense of belonging and reducing the feelings of isolation.

Creating safe and inclusive spaces within schools, workplaces, and communities is another important aspect of combating Hikikomori. By promoting a culture that values diversity, encourages open communication, and nurtures individual strengths, we can reduce the societal pressures that contribute to social withdrawal. Implementing support programs within educational institutions that prioritize mental health, offer counseling services, and foster a sense of community can help create a more supportive environment for students.

Additionally, vocational training and employment support programs can play a significant role in reintegrating Hikikomori individuals into society. By providing tailored assistance, such as skill development, career counseling, and job placement services, these programs can empower individuals to rebuild their lives and regain their independence.

In conclusion, the phenomenon of Hikikomori is a complex issue with far-reaching implications for individuals, families, and society as a whole. Understanding its multifaceted nature, including the underlying societal, cultural, and psychological factors, is essential in developing effective interventions. By promoting awareness, reducing stigma, and implementing comprehensive support systems, we can work towards creating a more inclusive and compassionate society that supports the mental well-being and reintegration of individuals affected by Hikikomori.

B) Understanding Social Isolation

Exploring the underlying causes and factors that contribute to social isolation, highlighting the psychological, societal, and cultural aspects involved.

In today's fast-paced and interconnected world, human beings have grown more connected than ever before. Social media platforms, instant messaging applications, and video conferencing tools have made it easy to engage with others globally. However, amidst this apparent connectivity, there exists a growing and concerning phenomenon known as social isolation.

Social isolation is a complex issue that affects individuals of all ages and backgrounds, hindering them from participating in meaningful social interactions and leading to a sense of loneliness and detachment from society. To fully grasp the intricacies of social isolation, it is important to delve into its underlying causes and factors, encompassing psychological, societal, and cultural aspects.

Psychologically, various factors contribute to social isolation. One significant factor is the prevalence of mental health disorders, such as depression, anxiety, and personality disorders. These conditions often manifest as a barrier to forming and maintaining relationships, making individuals feel detached and misunderstood. The stigma surrounding mental health issues can further exacerbate the problem, preventing individuals from seeking the support they need and perpetuating their isolation.

Additionally, low self-esteem and a lack of self-confidence can also contribute to social isolation. Individuals who doubt their own worth or fear judgment may withdraw from social interactions, as they perceive themselves as inadequate or unworthy of others' attention. These internal struggles become deeply ingrained and pose significant challenges to building meaningful connections with others.

Societal factors also play a crucial role in fostering social isolation. Modern society's emphasis on individualism and self-reliance has led to a decline in community-oriented activities and support networks. This shift influences the way people perceive and engage with others, as individual success and self-interest often take precedence over collective well-being. Consequently, individuals may feel disconnected from their communities and unable to form genuine relationships.

In addition, the rapid advancement of technology, while providing avenues for communication, has paradoxically contributed to social isolation. The allure of virtual interactions can create a false sense of connectedness, leading individuals to replace face-to-face interactions with online exchanges. This shift in communication dynamics can hinder social skills development, making it increasingly difficult for individuals to form real-life connections and navigate social environments.

Cultural factors further shape the experience of social isolation.

In some cultures, societal norms and expectations place excessive pressure on individuals to conform to specific roles or ideals. Deviation from these expectations can result in isolation and stigmatization. For instance, in collectivistic cultures, where conformity and social harmony are highly valued, individuals who fail to meet societal expectations or conform to traditional norms may face isolation and exclusion from their communities. Moreover, societal structures and inequalities, such as socioeconomic disparities and discrimination, can contribute to social isolation. Individuals from marginalized groups, such as racial or ethnic minorities, individuals with disabilities, or those in low-income communities, may face additional barriers to social inclusion. These systemic factors compound the challenges of social isolation, often leaving marginalized individuals with limited access to resources and opportunities for social engagement.

Understanding the underlying causes and factors of social isolation is crucial for developing effective strategies to overcome it. By acknowledging the psychological, societal, and cultural aspects involved, we can foster a greater sense of empathy and awareness within communities. Only through understanding can we begin to create environments that encourage inclusivity, genuine connections, and ultimately combat the detrimental effects of social isolation.

Cultural attitudes and societal norms greatly influence the experience of social isolation. Various cultures have different expectations and values that can contribute to feelings of detachment and exclusion. Understanding the cultural factors at play is essential to grasp the complexities of social isolation and to develop strategies for overcoming it.

In some cultures, societal norms and expectations exert significant pressure on individuals to conform to specific roles or ideals. Failure to meet these expectations can result in isolation and stigmatization. For example, in collectivistic cultures where conformity and social harmony are highly valued, individuals who deviate from societal norms or fail to meet the rigid expectations may face exclusion from their communities. This pressure to conform can be particularly challenging for those who do not fit the conventional norms or who wish to pursue their individuality, leading to a sense of isolation and alienation.

Furthermore, cultural differences in communication styles and social interaction can affect the prevalence of social isolation. In some cultures, interpersonal communication is more indirect and reliant on non-verbal cues, making it challenging for individuals from different cultural backgrounds to establish effective connections. These barriers may contribute to feelings of isolation, particularly for those from minority cultures living in societies with different dominant cultural norms.

Moreover, societal structures and inequalities, such as socioeconomic disparities and discrimination, contribute significantly to social isolation. Marginalized individuals, including racial or ethnic minorities, individuals with disabilities, or those in low-income communities, often encounter additional barriers to social inclusion. These systemic factors limit their access to resources and opportunities for social engagement, exacerbating their sense of isolation and disconnect from society. It is crucial to recognize these structural injustices and address them in order to foster inclusivity and equal social opportunities for everyone.

To overcome social isolation, it is imperative to create environments that encourage inclusivity and genuine connections. Communities should aim to provide spaces where individuals feel accepted, valued, and supported. This can involve promoting diversity and inclusivity through education and awareness initiatives, as well as challenging discriminatory behaviors and attitudes. By actively fostering empathy and understanding, communities can cultivate an environment that is more conducive to forming meaningful relationships and combating social isolation.

Mental health support systems also play a vital role in addressing social isolation. Encouraging open conversations about mental health, reducing stigma, and providing accessible mental health services can help individuals struggling with psychological challenges to seek the support they need. Creating safe and supportive spaces for individuals to discuss and address their mental health concerns is crucial to breaking the cycle of social isolation caused by mental health disorders.

Furthermore, society should focus on rebuilding community-oriented activities and support networks. By emphasizing the importance of collective well-being and facilitating opportunities for people to come together, communities can counterbalance the individualistic tendencies that contribute to social isolation. Engaging in community-based activities, volunteering, and participating in social groups can help individuals cultivate a sense of belonging and foster meaningful connections. These efforts not only combat social isolation but also encourage the formation of strong and supportive social networks.

In conclusion, cultural factors significantly shape the experience of social isolation. Societal expectations, cultural norms, and inequalities can contribute to feelings of detachment and exclusion. By recognizing and addressing these cultural factors, societies can work towards fostering inclusivity, understanding, and empathy. Developing a supportive environment where individuals feel accepted and valued, promoting mental health awareness and services, and rebuilding community-oriented activities can help overcome the detrimental effects of social isolation. It is through collective efforts and a commitment to inclusivity that we can create a society where no one feels isolated or disconnected.

CHAPTER 2: SIGNS AND SYMPTOMS
OF HIKIKOMORI

In order to address and overcome social isolation, it is imperative to understand the common signs and symptoms associated with Hikikomori behavior. By recognizing these indicators early on, individuals, families, and friends can take necessary steps to provide support and seek intervention for those affected.

Significant changes in behavior are often the first noticeable signs of Hikikomori. Individuals who withdraw from social interactions may exhibit increasingly introverted tendencies, preferring solitude over socializing. As their isolation intensifies, these individuals may display a lack of interest in activities they once enjoyed or a decline in academic or work performance. It is crucial to pay attention to such changes as they can be early warning signs of underlying issues.

The physical symptoms accompanying Hikikomori behavior vary from person to person but can manifest in numerous ways. Many individuals may experience changes in appetite or sleep patterns, which can lead to weight fluctuations and sleep disorders. Some may appear fatigued or lethargic, often spending prolonged periods confined to their rooms or homes. Furthermore, these individuals may neglect personal hygiene, leading to disheveled appearance and unkempt surroundings.

Emotional indicators can also provide insight into Hikikomori behavior. It is common for affected individuals to exhibit heightened anxiety or depression, which can manifest as frequent mood swings or emotional outbursts. Feelings of hopelessness, worthlessness, or a persistent sense of emptiness may permeate their thoughts and interactions. These emotional struggles can exacerbate their inclination towards isolation and reinforce their desire to withdraw further.

In addition to these individual signs, there are often observable changes in familial dynamics that accompany Hikikomori behavior. Family members may notice increased tension or conflict within the household as they struggle to understand and cope with the sudden withdrawal of their loved ones. Communication breakdowns become apparent, with affected individuals becoming increasingly unresponsive or defensive when engaging in conversations about their isolation. It is important for families to recognize these signs and address them promptly to facilitate open dialogue and support.

The impact of social isolation extends beyond the individual experiencing it, affecting their friends as well. Friends may observe a gradual detachment from social circles as those suffering from Hikikomori behavior become unresponsive to invitations or requests for outings. Their absence from social events, coupled with a lack of interest in maintaining friendships, can lead to strained relationships and a sense of helplessness among their peers. Recognizing these signs in friendships can aid in initiating conversations and offering support to those in need.

Understanding and identifying these signs and symptoms of Hikikomori behavior is crucial for early intervention. By recognizing these indicators, individuals, families, and friends can take the necessary steps to address the underlying issues and provide the support needed for recovery. In the second half of this chapter, we will explore various intervention strategies and resources available to help individuals overcome social isolation and reintegrate into society. Stay tuned for the next part, where we delve deeper into potential solutions and support systems.

Remember, the journey to understanding and overcoming Hikikomori behavior begins with recognition.

In the second half of this chapter, we will delve deeper into potential solutions and support systems for individuals experiencing Hikikomori behavior. Recognizing the signs and symptoms is just the first step towards understanding and overcoming social isolation.

But for now, let us explore the strategies and resources available to help individuals reintegrate into society.

One crucial aspect of addressing Hikikomori behavior is creating a supportive environment through open communication. Encouraging affected individuals to express their thoughts and emotions without fear of judgment or criticism is vital. It is essential for family members, friends, and professionals to actively listen and validate their experiences, offering empathy and understanding. By fostering a safe space for discussion, individuals with Hikikomori behavior may feel more comfortable opening up and seeking assistance.

Therapy and counseling play a pivotal role in the recovery process. Different therapeutic approaches can be tailored to meet the specific needs of individuals experiencing Hikikomori behavior. Cognitive-behavioral therapy (CBT) is often utilized to challenge and modify negative thoughts and behaviors, helping individuals develop healthier coping mechanisms. By identifying and restructuring distorted thinking patterns, CBT empowers individuals to navigate social situations with greater confidence and resilience.

Group therapy sessions can also offer tremendous benefits. Engaging in structured group settings allows individuals to share their experiences with others facing similar challenges, fostering a sense of belonging and understanding. Group therapy provides a platform for individuals to develop social skills, enhance self-esteem, and receive support from their peers who can relate to their struggles. Through the shared journey of recovery, participants can encourage and motivate one another, ultimately reducing feelings of isolation.

Additionally, incorporating art therapy and other creative outlets can provide a unique avenue for self-expression and self-discovery. Engaging in artistic endeavors such as painting, writing, or music can unlock emotions that may be difficult to verbalize. Art therapy allows individuals with Hikikomori behavior to explore their inner world, process their experiences, and communicate their feelings in a non-threatening and cathartic manner.

As with any mental health condition, medication may be prescribed in some cases to alleviate associated symptoms such as anxiety or depression. It is important to consult with a qualified healthcare professional to determine the appropriate medication and dosage based on an individual's specific needs. Medication should always be used in conjunction with therapy and other supportive interventions.

Reintegration into society is a significant milestone in overcoming Hikikomori behavior. Gradual exposure to social situations and environments can be achieved through a step-by-step approach. This may include engaging in structured activities such as volunteer work, joining clubs or organizations, or enrolling in educational or vocational programs. These structured activities not only provide opportunities for social interaction but also help individuals regain a sense of purpose and accomplishment.

Employment support programs tailored to the unique challenges faced by individuals with Hikikomori behavior can also facilitate their reintegration into the workforce. These programs often offer job training, skill development, and support in finding suitable employment opportunities. A gradual transition back into the workforce, with understanding employers and flexible work arrangements, can significantly contribute to an individual's success in overcoming social isolation.

Furthermore, the role of family and friends cannot be understated in supporting individuals with Hikikomori behavior. Patience, empathy, and ongoing encouragement are essential. Loved ones can assist by providing guidance and assistance in accessing available resources and accompanying individuals to therapy sessions or social outings. By standing by them on their path to recovery, family and friends can help restore trust, rebuild relationships, and reinforce positive social connections.

In conclusion, overcoming social isolation associated with Hikikomori behavior requires a multi-faceted approach that includes therapy, support groups, creative outlets, medication, if necessary, structured activities, and understanding employers. By utilizing these strategies and resources, individuals affected by Hikikomori behavior can gradually regain their confidence, develop social skills, and reintegrate into society. Each step on this journey requires patience, perseverance, and the unwavering support of loved ones and professionals. Together, we can pave the way for a brighter, more socially connected future.

CHAPTER 3: THE EFFECTS OF HIKIKOMORI ON MENTAL HEALTH

Examining the impact of social isolation on mental health, discussing common mental health disorders associated with Hikikomori, and the importance of seeking professional help.

Social isolation and its effects on mental well-being have become increasingly prevalent in today's society. One particular phenomenon, known as Hikikomori, has garnered attention for its profound impact on individuals' mental health. Hikikomori refers to a state of extreme social withdrawal, where individuals voluntarily isolate themselves from society for extended periods, often years on end. As we delve into this chapter, we will explore the devastating effects of Hikikomori on mental health, shed light on the common mental health disorders associated with this phenomenon, and emphasize the importance of seeking professional help.

Social isolation, by its very nature, creates a breeding ground for various mental health challenges. Hikikomori individuals find themselves trapped in a self-imposed cocoon, cut off from social interactions and lacking meaningful connections. This isolation often leads to a decline in mental and emotional well-being. Loneliness, despair, and a deep sense of hopelessness become constant companions for those affected by Hikikomori. The toll on their mental health can be severe.

One of the most prevalent mental health disorders linked to Hikikomori is depression. The prolonged solitude and lack of human interaction often exacerbate pre-existing depressive tendencies, and may even trigger this debilitating condition in vulnerable individuals. The weight of isolation, coupled with the absence of a supportive network, can lead to an overwhelming sense of sadness, loss of interest, and persistent feelings of worthlessness. Without the necessary intervention, depression can spiral into a cycle that is difficult to break free from.

Anxiety disorders frequently coexist with Hikikomori, further intensifying the distress experienced by affected individuals. The constant fear of judgment, humiliation, or rejection prevents them from seeking social contact, perpetuating their isolation. Generalized anxiety disorder, social anxiety disorder, and panic disorder are often observed in Hikikomori cases. The constant anticipation of negative outcomes and the inability to cope with everyday stressors contribute to the deterioration of mental well-being.

Moreover, Hikikomori individuals are also at a heightened risk of developing obsessive-compulsive disorder (OCD). The lack of external stimuli might lead to a reliance on repetitive actions and rituals as a means of regaining control or mitigating anxiety. These individuals find solace in their structured routines, as it provides them with a semblance of stability amidst the chaos of their isolated realities. However, this reliance on rituals can further reinforce their withdrawal from society, perpetuating the cycle of Hikikomori and exacerbating their mental health issues.

While Hikikomori takes a tremendous toll on mental health, it is crucial to emphasize the importance of seeking professional help. Mental health professionals play a pivotal role in providing support, guidance, and effective treatment modalities tailored specifically for individuals affected by Hikikomori. Therapeutic interventions such as cognitive-behavioral therapy (CBT), exposure therapy, and medication management have demonstrated promising results in addressing the underlying causes of social withdrawal and associated mental health disorders.

However, the road to recovery may not always be smooth. The process of encouraging Hikikomori individuals to seek help can be challenging, as they might feel immense fear, shame, or resistance towards breaking free from their isolation. It is, therefore, essential to approach them with compassion, understanding, and the knowledge that recovery is possible.

In conclusion, the effects of Hikikomori on mental health are profound, with depression, anxiety disorders, and OCD being some of the common challenges faced by those in extreme social isolation. Recognizing the debilitating impacts of this phenomenon is crucial in fostering understanding and empathy towards affected individuals. Seeking professional help and intervention is vital in overcoming these mental health hurdles and finding a path towards reintegration into society. In the forthcoming second half of this chapter, we will explore success stories and effective strategies utilized in aiding Hikikomori individuals on their journey to recovery. But for now, the path to healing lies in acknowledging the immense struggle faced by those isolated from the world around them, and ensuring they know they are not alone.As we explore the second half of this chapter, we will delve deeper into success stories and effective strategies utilized in aiding Hikikomori individuals on their journey to recovery. These stories provide hope, encouragement, and valuable insights into overcoming the challenges posed by extreme social isolation.

One important aspect of addressing Hikikomori and its effects on mental health is the role of support networks. When individuals are trapped in the depths of self-imposed isolation, it becomes crucial to establish connections and build a foundation for recovery. Family members, friends, and mental health professionals play a vital role in extending their support and creating a safe environment conducive to healing. These individuals can offer empathy, understanding, and encouragement that helps break the barriers of isolation. By fostering an atmosphere of trust and acceptance, they provide the necessary motivation for Hikikomori individuals to take their first steps towards reintegration into society.

One effective strategy in aiding Hikikomori individuals is the use of gradual exposure therapy. This therapy involves gently introducing individuals to social situations in a controlled and supportive manner. By gradually increasing the intensity and duration of these exposures, individuals are able to overcome their fears and anxieties associated with social interactions. The guidance of mental health professionals in this process is essential, as they can tailor the exposure therapy to meet the specific needs and challenges faced by each individual.

Another effective approach is the implementation of cognitive-behavioral therapy (CBT). CBT focuses on identifying and challenging negative thought patterns and behaviors associated with social withdrawal. By working collaboratively with a therapist, Hikikomori individuals can gain a better understanding of their emotions and develop healthy coping mechanisms to overcome their social anxieties. Through cognitive restructuring and the development of a more positive mindset, individuals can gradually regain their confidence and improve their overall mental well-being.

In some cases, medication management may also be beneficial in addressing underlying mental health disorders associated with Hikikomori. Antidepressants or anti-anxiety medications, when prescribed by a qualified psychiatrist, can help alleviate symptoms and create a stable foundation for therapy and rehabilitation.

It is important, however, that medication is used as part of a comprehensive treatment plan that includes therapy and support systems, as it is not a standalone solution.

Furthermore, community support programs have emerged as valuable resources for Hikikomori individuals seeking recovery. These programs provide a non-judgmental, understanding environment where individuals can meet others facing similar struggles. Through activities, group therapy sessions, and shared experiences, participants can foster meaningful connections and develop skills to reintegrate into society. Such programs offer practical assistance, emotional support, and a sense of belonging that aids individuals in regaining their self-confidence and rebuilding their social lives.

While the journey to recovery may be challenging, it is essential to recognize that progress can be made. The stories of individuals who have successfully overcome Hikikomori provide inspiration and evidence that healing is possible. By embracing a comprehensive treatment approach, Hikikomori individuals can learn to manage their mental health challenges, develop healthy coping mechanisms, and rebuild their lives.

In conclusion, the second half of this chapter has shed light on the transformative power of support networks, gradual exposure therapy, cognitive-behavioral therapy, medication management, and community support programs in aiding Hikikomori individuals on their path to recovery. These strategies, in conjunction with the unwavering encouragement and understanding from their loved ones and mental health professionals, can help individuals break free from the chains of extreme social withdrawal. It is crucial for society to recognize the profound impact of Hikikomori on mental health and ensure that necessary resources and support are available to those affected. With these tools and a renewed sense of hope, we can collectively combat social isolation and create a more empathetic and inclusive society.

CHAPTER 4: UNDERSTANDING THE ROLE OF FAMILY AND RELATIONSHIPS

Exploring the influence of family dynamics and relationship patterns on the development and persistence of Hikikomori behavior, offering strategies for building healthier family connections.

Social isolation, particularly the condition known as Hikikomori, affects numerous individuals worldwide. This phenomenon, characterized by extreme withdrawal from social contact, can have severe consequences for those experiencing it as well as their families. In order to better comprehend the reasons behind this behavior, it is imperative to examine the role of family dynamics and relationship patterns.

Family plays a pivotal role in shaping an individual's development and emotional well-being. Within the family unit, various dynamics and patterns emerge, which significantly impact a person's social skills, coping mechanisms, and overall mental health. These aspects can either contribute to or alleviate the risk of Hikikomori behavior.

One crucial influence on Hikikomori development is the family communication style. Communication patterns within the family can vary greatly, ranging from open and supportive to closed and conflict-ridden. Research has shown that individuals raised in families with poor communication tend to struggle with expressing their feelings, needs, and concerns. This lack of effective communication often leads to misunderstandings, emotional distance, and a reduced sense of belonging.

Furthermore, family relationships characterized by high levels of conflict and tension can significantly contribute to the onset of Hikikomori behavior. Constant family disputes, whether verbal or physical, create an unhealthy environment that undermines emotional security and stability. When individuals are continuously exposed to hostile interactions, feelings of fear and anxiety arise, eroding their trust in others and their ability to form meaningful connections.

Additionally, parental attitudes and expectations exert a considerable influence on a person's Hikikomori tendencies. In some instances, parents may inadvertently contribute to their child's withdrawal from society by putting excessive pressure on them to succeed academically or conform to societal norms. The weight of unrealistically high expectations can foster feelings of inadequacy and fear of failure, pushing individuals towards isolation as a retreat from judgment and disappointment.

It is important to acknowledge that familial factors alone cannot solely account for the complex nature of Hikikomori behavior. Numerous societal, cultural, and individual elements intertwine, contributing to its development. Nevertheless, exploring and understanding the influence of family dynamics on this phenomenon provides a crucial starting point for intervention and recovery.

To address Hikikomori and foster healthier family connections, several strategies can be implemented. First and foremost, fostering open communication is paramount. Encouraging family members to express their thoughts and emotions in a safe and supportive environment can help prevent miscommunication and emotional distance. Building effective communication skills can promote understanding, empathy, and a sense of belonging, creating a familial atmosphere conducive to healthy emotional development.

Moreover, it is essential for families to cultivate an environment of emotional security and trust. By reducing conflict and tension, individuals will feel safer within the family unit, lowering their likelihood of seeking solace in isolation. This can be achieved through family therapy, conflict resolution techniques, and creating a home environment that prioritizes mutual respect and understanding.

In addition to working on family dynamics, it is vital to address parental expectations. Parents should encourage their children to explore their own unique paths, valuing personal growth and individuality over societal expectations. By fostering a sense of self-worth and autonomy, families can empower individuals to navigate challenges and setbacks without retreating into isolation.

Understanding the critical role of family dynamics and relationship patterns provides valuable insights into the development and persistence of Hikikomori behavior. By implementing strategies that foster open communication, emotional security, and realistic expectations, families can play a pivotal role in supporting individuals in their journey towards overcoming social isolation.

The Influence of Emotional Support in Overcoming Hikikomori Behavior

Understanding the critical role of family dynamics and relationship patterns provides valuable insights into the development and persistence of Hikikomori behavior. By implementing strategies that foster open communication, emotional security, and realistic expectations, families can play a pivotal role in supporting individuals in their journey towards overcoming social isolation.

One crucial aspect in building healthier family connections and assisting individuals in their recovery from Hikikomori behavior is the presence of emotional support within the family. Emotional support refers to the availability of affection, empathy, and understanding from family members, which plays a fundamental role in promoting resilience and psychological well-being.

Research has consistently demonstrated the positive impact of emotional support on mental health outcomes.

Individuals who perceive higher levels of support from their families tend to experience reduced levels of anxiety, depression, and social withdrawal. Within the context of Hikikomori, emotional support from family members can be a vital lifeline, offering the reassurance and encouragement needed to face the challenges of social reintegration.

To cultivate emotional support within the family, it is important for family members to actively listen and validate each other's experiences and emotions. Empathy and genuine understanding can help create an atmosphere of acceptance and compassion, diminishing feelings of isolation and alienation.

It is also essential to provide Hikikomori individuals with the opportunity to voice their concerns and actively participate in decision-making processes that affect them. By involving them in family discussions and allowing them to express their thoughts and opinions, individuals can regain a sense of control and agency in their lives. This empowerment is crucial in motivating individuals to overcome their fears and take steps towards reconnecting with others.

Furthermore, families can benefit from seeking external support in the form of therapy or support groups. Professional counseling can provide families with guidance on how to navigate the challenges associated with Hikikomori behavior and develop effective coping strategies. Support groups create a space for families to connect with others who share similar experiences, fostering a sense of solidarity and understanding.

In addition to emotional support, the provision of social outlets and opportunities for social engagement is paramount in reintegrating Hikikomori individuals into society. Gradual exposure to social situations, such as joining clubs or engaging in volunteer work, can help individuals build their confidence and social skills. Families can support this process by encouraging participation in activities that align with their interests and providing ongoing encouragement and assistance.

However, it is essential to approach social reintegration gradually and with sensitivity. Pushing individuals too quickly or excessively may result in heightened anxiety and resistance. Patience and understanding, paired with a supportive environment, are key factors in successfully overcoming Hikikomori behavior.

To maintain progress and prevent relapse, families must prioritize ongoing communication and emotional support even after individuals have reintegrated into society. Periodically checking in with family members, ensuring their emotional needs are being met, and addressing any emerging challenges promptly are all part of cultivating a healthy and supportive family environment.

In conclusion, the second half of Chapter 5 has explored the significance of emotional support and social reintegration in overcoming Hikikomori behavior. Emotional support from family members can serve as a crucial resource for individuals during their journey towards recovery. By fostering open communication, actively listening, validating emotions, seeking external support, and gradually aiding social reintegration, families can play an essential role in helping individuals overcome social isolation. Providing continued emotional support and maintaining open lines of communication are important factors in nurturing long-term recovery.

CHAPTER 5: SOCIETAL AND CULTURAL FACTORS CONTRIBUTING TO HIKIKOMORI

Investigating the social and cultural factors that contribute to the emergence and prevalence of Hikikomori, shedding light on the impact of societal pressures and expectations.

In order to fully understand the phenomenon of Hikikomori, it is essential to dive into the complex web of societal and cultural factors that contribute to its emergence and prevalence. Hikikomori, a term originating from Japan, refers to the withdrawal and social isolation experienced by individuals who choose to retreat from society, often for an extended period of time. While the manifestation of Hikikomori may differ across cultures, it is undeniable that various societal and cultural aspects play a significant role in its development.

One of the fundamental drivers of Hikikomori is the immense pressure and high expectations imposed by society. Throughout many cultures, societal norms create an atmosphere where individuals are constantly striving to meet the standards set by their families, peers, and communities. From a young age, children are burdened with an array of expectations, ranging from excelling academically to conforming to societal ideals of success. The relentless pursuit of excellence often leads to immense stress and burnout, forcing individuals into seclusion as a means of escape.

Furthermore, cultural collectivism prevalent in many societies can intensify the pressure to conform. In societies that value group harmony and interconnectedness, the fear of social judgment and ostracization can push individuals into isolation. The fear of disappointing one's family or community, and the associated stigma and shame, can be paralyzing. As a result, individuals may find solace in the confines of their homes, shunning social interaction altogether.

Additionally, the ever-increasing influence of technology and social media has had a profound impact on the prevalence of Hikikomori. The advent of virtual connectivity has simultaneously provided an escape from face-to-face social interaction and created an alternative realm where individuals can feel a sense of belonging without the anxiety-inducing pressures of physical interaction. Online communities and gaming platforms provide a refuge for Hikikomori individuals, allowing them to form connections and establish identities separate from their real-life experiences.

Moreover, the rapid pace of technological advancement and its integration into daily life has altered societal dynamics, further contributing to social isolation. As technology becomes an integral part of how individuals communicate and interact, there is a decrease in the need for physical presence. The convenience and anonymity of online interactions can gradually erode social skills, making it increasingly challenging for Hikikomori individuals to reintegrate into society. The lure of the digital world becomes stronger, exacerbating the isolation experienced by these individuals.

In conclusion, societal and cultural factors significantly contribute to the emergence and prevalence of Hikikomori. The immense pressure to meet societal expectations, the influence of cultural collectivism, and the impact of technology and social media all intertwine to create an environment conducive to social withdrawal. Understanding these factors is crucial in developing effective strategies to address and support individuals who experience Hikikomori. By recognizing the detrimental effects of societal pressures and expectations, we can work towards fostering a more compassionate and understanding society that values individual well-being over rigid standards of success.

Furthermore, the prevalence of hikikomori can also be attributed to the breakdown of traditional community structures and support systems. In many societies, the shift towards modernization and urbanization has led to the erosion of close-knit communities and intergenerational relationships. As individuals become more disconnected from their neighbors and extended families, the sense of belonging and social support diminishes. This isolation can leave individuals feeling alienated and alone, exacerbating their inclination toward withdrawal from society.

Moreover, the fast-paced and competitive nature of modern society plays a significant role in the development of hikikomori. As globalization and technological advancements continue to reshape the world, individuals are faced with ever-increasing demands and expectations. The constant pursuit of success and the pressures associated with it can leave individuals feeling overwhelmed and powerless. This sense of powerlessness can contribute to the desire to escape and withdraw from society entirely.

In addition to societal pressures, the cultural emphasis on conformity can also contribute to the emergence of hikikomori. In many cultures, particularly those with strong collectivist values, the societal norms and expectations can be stifling. The fear of deviating from societal norms or bringing shame upon oneself or one's family can be paralyzing, pushing individuals to seek refuge in isolation. The weight of these expectations, combined with the potential consequences of failing to meet them, can create a tremendous sense of pressure and anxiety.

Furthermore, the stigmatization and misconceptions surrounding mental health and social withdrawal can significantly impact individuals experiencing hikikomori. In many societies, mental health issues are still highly stigmatized and often misunderstood. The lack of understanding and support for individuals struggling with their mental well-being can exacerbate their isolation and discourage seeking help. This results in a vicious cycle, further perpetuating the hikikomori phenomenon.

It is important to acknowledge that hikikomori is not

solely limited to Japan or any specific culture. While the manifestations and terminology may vary, social withdrawal and isolation can be observed across different societies and geographies. In Western cultures, for instance, similar phenomena are often referred to as "social recluses" or "hermits." This suggests that societal and cultural factors contributing to withdrawal from society transcend national boundaries.

Efforts to address and support individuals experiencing hikikomori must consider the interplay between societal pressures, cultural expectations, and individual well-being. Interventions aimed at combating hikikomori should involve a multi-dimensional approach encompassing mental health support, community building, and targeted educational initiatives.

First and foremost, destigmatizing mental health and providing accessible and culturally sensitive mental health resources is crucial. Raising awareness and promoting understanding of hikikomori as a legitimate mental health concern will encourage individuals to seek help without fear of judgment or shame. It is essential to establish a supportive and empathetic environment where individuals experiencing hikikomori can openly discuss their struggles and find appropriate assistance.

Additionally, building supportive communities can play a pivotal role in reintegrating individuals back into society. Creating spaces where individuals can connect with like-minded peers, share experiences, and foster a sense of belonging can significantly contribute to their overall well-being. Community-based projects, support groups, and mentorship programs can provide the necessary social support systems to mitigate feelings of isolation and encourage re-engagement with society.

Furthermore, addressing societal pressures and expectations is essential to prevent the emergence of hikikomori. Shifting societal attitudes towards success and encouraging a more holistic understanding of individual well-being can alleviate the intense pressure faced by individuals. Promoting a healthier work-life balance, redefining notions of success, and providing alternative paths to fulfillment can help individuals navigate the societal demands without resorting to withdrawal.

Lastly, integrating technology and digital platforms as tools for connection rather than avoidance is crucial. Encouraging responsible and balanced use of technology while promoting face-to-face interactions can help individuals develop and maintain social skills necessary for healthy engagement with the world. By harnessing the potential of technology and social media in facilitating social connections and support networks, we can offer individuals experiencing hikikomori a bridge between isolation and integration.

In conclusion, the second half of this chapter has explored additional societal and cultural factors contributing to the prevalence of hikikomori. The breakdown of community structures, the pressures of modernization, cultural conformity, and the stigmatization of mental health all play a significant role. By recognizing these factors and implementing comprehensive strategies that address mental health, build supportive communities, challenge societal expectations, and effectively utilize technology, we can work towards alleviating the burden of hikikomori and creating a more inclusive and understanding society.

CHAPTER 6: APPROACHES TO INTERVENTION AND TREATMENT

Social isolation can have devastating effects on individuals, leading to a condition known as Hikikomori. In this chapter, we will explore various intervention and treatment approaches that can help individuals understand and overcome this phenomenon. By providing a comprehensive overview of therapy, medication, group support, and alternative methods for promoting recovery, we aim to shed light on the potential paths towards a healthier and happier life for those affected by Hikikomori.

Therapy plays a crucial role in the treatment of Hikikomori, as it offers individuals an opportunity to explore their thoughts, emotions, and behaviors in a safe and confidential environment. Cognitive-Behavioral Therapy (CBT) is often employed as it focuses on identifying and challenging negative thought patterns and behaviors that contribute to social isolation. By working with a therapist, individuals can develop healthier coping mechanisms, improve their self-esteem, and gradually reintegrate into society.

Another approach worth considering is medication, particularly in cases where underlying mental health conditions, such as anxiety or depression, coexist with Hikikomori. Antidepressant and anti-anxiety medications can help alleviate symptoms, allowing individuals to engage in therapeutic interventions more effectively. However, it is important to note that medication alone is not a cure, but rather a complementary tool to support overall recovery.

Group support has proven to be invaluable for individuals experiencing social isolation. Group therapy allows individuals to connect with others who have similar experiences, creating an understanding and non-judgmental environment. Through sharing their stories, individuals can gain insight, empathy, and practical advice on how to overcome Hikikomori. Moreover, group support provides a sense of belonging and helps individuals realize that they are not alone in their struggles.

In addition to traditional approaches, alternative methods can be considered to enhance the recovery process for Hikikomori. These approaches include art therapy, music therapy, nature-based therapies, and animal-assisted therapy. Art therapy, for instance, allows individuals to express themselves creatively, bridging the gap between their emotions and external world. Music therapy offers a similar avenue for self-expression and emotional release. Nature-based therapies, on the other hand, enable individuals to reconnect with the natural world, fostering a sense of peace and tranquility. Lastly, animal-assisted therapy involves engaging with animals to promote emotional well-being and social connection.

While these approaches offer potential interventions for Hikikomori, it is important to customize treatment plans to the individual's specific needs and preferences. Optimal outcomes are achieved when combining multiple approaches based on the individual's condition, severity of social isolation, underlying factors, and personal goals.

By implementing various interventions and treatment approaches, we can provide individuals with the tools they need to overcome social isolation and lead fulfilling lives. In the second half of this chapter, we will delve deeper into the nuances of each approach and explore case studies that highlight their effectiveness. Through continued research and understanding, we can pave the way for a future where Hikikomori becomes a thing of the past.

Stay tuned for the next part, where we will uncover more insights and provide practical examples of successful interventions in Hikikomori cases. The journey to understanding and overcoming social isolation is just beginning, and together, we can make a difference.

Next we will delve deeper into the nuances of each intervention and treatment approach for Hikikomori, exploring case studies that highlight their effectiveness. Through these practical examples, we can gain valuable insights into successful interventions and further understand the journey to understanding and overcoming social isolation.

One intervention approach that has shown promising results in the treatment of Hikikomori is Cognitive-Behavioral Therapy (CBT). This therapy not only helps individuals identify and challenge negative thought patterns and behaviors that contribute to social isolation but also provides practical tools to develop healthier coping mechanisms and improve self-esteem. Case studies have demonstrated that individuals engaged in CBT gradually re-integrate into society, regain independence, and experience an improvement in their overall well-being.

In a case study conducted with a 29-year-old individual named Akihiro, who had been socially isolated for six years, CBT helped him gain a deeper understanding of his fear of rejection and anxieties in social situations. Through therapy sessions, Akihiro was able to challenge his distorted beliefs and develop more realistic and positive thinking patterns. With the guidance of a therapist and the implementation of exposure exercises, Akihiro began to attend social events and gradually build social connections. Over time, he reported a significant reduction in his social anxiety and an improvement in his ability to navigate social interactions.

Another intervention that complements therapeutic approaches is the use of medication, particularly in cases where individuals with Hikikomori have underlying mental health conditions such as anxiety or depression. Antidepressant and anti-anxiety medications can help alleviate symptoms, making it easier for individuals to engage in therapeutic interventions effectively. However, it's important to note that medication alone is not a cure for Hikikomori but rather a supportive tool in the overall treatment plan.

In a case study involving a 36-year-old individual named Hiroshi, who had been socially isolated for eight years and experienced severe depression, the combination of medication and therapy proved highly beneficial. Hiroshi's psychiatrist prescribed an antidepressant that helped stabilize his mood and reduce his symptoms of depression. With the support of therapy, Hiroshi was able to address the underlying issues contributing to his social isolation, develop healthier coping strategies, and gradually integrate back into society. This case study emphasizes the importance of customized treatment plans that may involve both medication and therapy for individuals with coexisting mental health conditions.

Group support is another vital intervention approach in the treatment of Hikikomori. By connecting with others who have similar experiences, individuals can gain insight, empathy, and practical advice on how to overcome their isolation. Group therapy provides a safe and non-judgmental environment where individuals can share their stories, learn from one another, and develop a sense of belonging. Research has shown that individuals engaged in group therapy experience a reduction in feelings of loneliness and an increase in social connectedness.

A case study involving a group therapy program implemented in a community center highlights the effectiveness of this intervention approach. The program included ten individuals with varying degrees of social isolation. Over the course of twelve weeks, participants engaged in group therapy sessions that focused on building social skills, improving self-esteem, and fostering peer support. By the end of the program, participants reported a significant reduction in their levels of isolation and an increase in their ability to engage in social activities. This case study exemplifies the power of group support in addressing the challenges associated with Hikikomori.

In addition to traditional approaches, alternative methods can also be considered to enhance the recovery process for individuals with Hikikomori. Art therapy, for instance, provides a creative outlet for self-expression and emotional release. Through various art modalities, individuals can explore their feelings, thoughts, and experiences, allowing them to bridge the gap between their internal world and external reality.

A case study involving a 23-year-old individual named Yuki demonstrates the therapeutic potential of art therapy. Yuki, who had been socially isolated for four years, began attending art therapy sessions as part of her treatment plan. Through painting and drawing, Yuki was able to express her emotions, communicate her experiences, and gain a sense of agency over her life. The art therapy sessions helped her develop a stronger sense of self and gradually regain confidence in her ability to connect with others.

Music therapy also offers an alternative approach to promoting recovery from social isolation. By engaging in musical activities, individuals can tap into their emotions, express themselves creatively, and experience a sense of connection. Whether through playing an instrument, singing, or listening to music, music therapy provides a unique opportunity for individuals to communicate and connect with others on a different level.

An illustrative case study involving a 32-year-old individual named Takumi reveals the transformative potential of music therapy. Takumi, who had been socially isolated for three years, started participating in group music therapy sessions. Through collaborative music-making and improvisation, Takumi developed social skills, gained confidence in his abilities, and discovered a newfound sense of belonging. The rhythmic and melodic aspects of music facilitated communication among the group members, ultimately fostering a supportive and inclusive environment.

Nature-based therapies have demonstrated positive outcomes in the treatment of Hikikomori. By immersing individuals in natural environments and engaging in activities such as gardening, hiking, or wilderness therapy, they can experience a sense of peace, calm, and connectedness with the world around them. Nature-based therapies provide a space for reflection, rejuvenation, and the development of a deeper appreciation for the beauty of the natural world.

A case study involving a 27-year-old individual named Emi showcases the effectiveness of nature-based therapy. Emi, who had been socially isolated for seven years, began attending wilderness therapy sessions as part of her treatment plan. Through guided hikes, outdoor activities, and reflection exercises in nature, Emi gradually developed a more positive outlook on her life and an enhanced connection with the world. This case study underscores the therapeutic potential of connecting with nature in supporting individuals with Hikikomori on their journey towards recovery.

Lastly, animal-assisted therapy provides a unique and effective approach to promoting emotional well-being and social connection. By interacting with animals such as dogs, cats, or horses, individuals can experience feelings of comfort, companionship, and unconditional acceptance. Animal-assisted therapy can help individuals reduce feelings of isolation, improve social skills, foster empathy, and develop a sense of responsibility. A case study involving a 31-year-old individual named Kaori highlights the transformative impact of animal-assisted therapy. Kaori, who had been socially isolated for five years, began attending equine therapy sessions. Through engaging with horses, Kaori developed a sense of trust, improved her communication skills, and learned to establish healthy boundaries in relationships. The gentle nature of the horses provided a safe and non-judgmental environment where Kaori could practice these newfound skills and experience a sense of connection.

In conclusion, the second half of this chapter has explored various intervention and treatment approaches for Hikikomori, including Cognitive-Behavioral Therapy, medication, group support, and alternative methods such as art therapy, music therapy, nature-based therapies, and animal-assisted therapy. Through case studies, we have witnessed the transformative potential of these approaches in helping individuals overcome social isolation and reconnect with society.

By customizing treatment plans to meet individuals' specific needs and preferences, we can empower them with the tools they need to embark on a path towards a healthier and happier life. The journey to understanding and overcoming social isolation continues, and with continued research and understanding, we can make a meaningful difference in the lives of those affected by Hikikomori.

CHAPTER 7: BUILDING SUPPORTIVE COMMUNITIES

In the journey towards understanding and overcoming hikikomori, the significance of community support cannot be overstated. Human beings are social creatures, and the desire for connection and belonging is inherent within us all. When individuals become trapped in the cycle of social isolation, it is the power of supportive communities that can provide the foundation for their reintegration.

Organizations play a crucial role in fostering social reintegration and supporting individuals struggling with hikikomori. These organizations often act as a bridge, connecting isolated individuals with the resources, guidance, and support they need to rebuild their lives. From providing counseling services and therapy sessions to organizing social activities and skill development programs, these organizations form the backbone of community-based intervention.

One such organization is the Hikikomori Support Network. Founded by a group of dedicated professionals and hikikomori survivors themselves, their primary aim is to create a safe space where individuals can share their experiences, fears, and frustrations. By offering a supportive environment, where non-judgmental conversations can take place, these organizations help hikikomori individuals gradually rebuild their social skills, self-confidence, and sense of belonging.

Moreover, online platforms have emerged as powerful tools for creating virtual communities that reach out to hikikomori individuals. These platforms provide a sanctuary for individuals who may find it challenging to engage in face-to-face interactions.

Online forums and chat groups allow hikikomori individuals to communicate anonymously, share their stories, and offer advice to one another. These digital communities serve as a lifeline for those who feel trapped within the confines of their physical surroundings, enabling them to connect with others who understand their struggles.

While organizations and online platforms play an important role, peer networks can have a significant impact in promoting social reintegration. Peers who have experienced or are still experiencing hikikomori can provide unique insights, empathy, and support to those embarking on their journey to overcome social isolation. Peer-led support groups offer a sense of community, understanding, and hope as individuals engage in open discussions about their shared experiences. These networks empower individuals by demonstrating that recovery and reintegration are indeed possible.

Building supportive communities requires a multi-faceted approach. It involves addressing the underlying issues that contribute to hikikomori, such as mental health challenges, societal pressures, and lack of opportunities. Furthermore, it necessitates breaking down stigmas associated with social withdrawal and fostering empathy and understanding among individuals in the wider community.

As we explore the power of community support in overcoming hikikomori, it is clear that no single approach can fit every situation. Each individual struggling with social isolation has a unique set of circumstances and needs. Therefore, a comprehensive and inclusive strategy that combines the efforts of organizations, online platforms, and peer networks is essential.

The second part of this chapter will dive deeper into the specific strategies employed by these supportive communities, showcasing real-life stories of individuals who have successfully overcome hikikomori and highlighting the diverse approaches that can contribute to social reintegration. By learning from these experiences, we can glean valuable insights into the different paths towards recovery and, ultimately, the power of community in transforming lives.

Now we will delve deeper into the specific strategies employed by supportive communities, it becomes evident that overcoming hikikomori requires a holistic approach that addresses diverse aspects of an individual's life. Real-life stories of individuals who have successfully navigated the journey out of social isolation serve as powerful reminders of the transformative power of community support.

One important aspect of building supportive communities is the provision of mental health services.

Many hikikomori individuals experience underlying mental health challenges that contribute to their social withdrawal. By offering counseling services, therapy sessions, and psychiatric support, organizations pave the way for individuals to address their psychological well-being. These interventions not only provide much-needed guidance and coping mechanisms but also break down the stigma associated with seeking mental health assistance.

Furthermore, organizations prioritize skill development programs to help individuals enhance their self-esteem and acquire practical abilities that can facilitate their reintegration. These programs may include vocational training, education opportunities, and job placement assistance. By empowering hikikomori individuals with valuable skills, organizations foster their independence and enable them to navigate and contribute to society.

In addition to traditional organizations, online platforms continue to play a crucial role in supporting those experiencing hikikomori. Virtual communities offer a space for individuals who face difficulties in engaging in face-to-face interactions due to anxiety or physical limitations. These platforms facilitate connection, information-sharing, and emotional support. Online forums and chat groups allow individuals to communicate anonymously, offering a lifeline for those feeling trapped within the confines of their physical surroundings.

Digital communities also provide opportunities for hikikomori individuals to engage in creative pursuits and discover new interests. Writing, art, music, and gaming communities provide a means for self-expression and exploration in a safe and non-judgmental environment. By fostering creativity and offering avenues for personal growth, these platforms can inspire individuals to gradually open up and explore the possibility of social reintegration.

While organizations and online platforms are essential, peer networks remain a cornerstone of building supportive communities. Peers who have experienced or are currently facing hikikomori can offer unique insights and empathy. Peer-led support groups provide a sense of community, understanding, and hope. Through open discussions about shared experiences, individuals feel validated and motivated to overcome social isolation.

The role of peer networks extends beyond support groups. Peer mentors can play an integral role in guiding and motivating hikikomori individuals throughout their journey. These mentors, having successfully overcome their own isolation, understand the challenges firsthand and serve as living proof that reintegration is possible. The bonds formed within these relationships cultivate a sense of trust and provide the necessary encouragement for individuals to take steps towards reconnecting with society.

To facilitate the reintegration process effectively, it is crucial to address societal stigmas associated with social withdrawal and foster empathy and understanding within the wider community. Education and awareness campaigns can help dispel the misconceptions surrounding hikikomori, thereby encouraging empathy and reducing judgment. By fostering an inclusive and accepting society, individuals who have experienced social isolation can find solace and support, ultimately aiding their reintegration efforts.

In conclusion, understanding and overcoming hikikomori necessitates the establishment of supportive communities that address the multifaceted nature of social isolation. Through organizations, online platforms, and peer networks, individuals are provided with invaluable resources, guidance, and empathy. By prioritizing mental health services, skill development, and the breaking down of societal stigmas, these communities foster a sense of belonging and empowerment.

As we absorb the valuable lessons and insights from real-life experiences showcased throughout this chapter, we witness the transformative power of community in the lives of hikikomori individuals. By recognizing the uniqueness of each individual's circumstances and needs, we come to appreciate the importance of a comprehensive and inclusive strategy. The path to recovery is diverse, and by embracing various approaches, we can collectively strive towards a society that values connection, understanding, and support for all.

CHAPTER 8: STRATEGIES FOR REINTEGRATION INTO SOCIETY

In the journey towards reintegration into society, individuals who have experienced social isolation face unique challenges. However, with the right strategies and practical advice, it is possible to overcome these obstacles and forge a path towards a more fulfilling and connected life. This chapter aims to provide valuable insights and actionable steps for individuals who are ready to embark on this transformative journey.

BUILDING SKILLS: A FOUNDATION
FOR REINTEGRATION

One of the crucial aspects of successfully reintegrating into society is developing essential skills that may have been neglected during periods of social isolation. These skills can vary from basic interpersonal communication to more advanced abilities like problem-solving or emotional intelligence. By focusing on skill-building, individuals can enhance their confidence and efficacy in various social situations.

First and foremost, it is important to recognize that these skills can be developed and improved with practice. Don't be discouraged if initially interactions feel uncomfortable or if certain situations trigger anxiety. Begin by starting small and gradually increase the level of difficulty. For example, initiating conversations with close friends or family members can be a good starting point to practice active listening and effective communication skills.

In addition, seeking professional help from therapists, counselors, or social workers can be immensely beneficial. These professionals can provide personalized guidance and support, tailored to an individual's specific needs. They may even offer workshops or group therapy sessions that facilitate skill development through role-playing exercises, group discussions, and other interactive activities.

SETTING REALISTIC GOALS: MAPPING THE WAY FORWARD

To ensure progress towards successful reintegration, setting realistic goals is crucial. As individuals work towards their desired outcomes, they can experience a sense of purpose, achievement, and direction. However, it is important to approach goal-setting with patience and self-compassion.

When setting goals, consider both short-term and long-term objectives. Short-term goals can act as stepping stones towards larger aspirations, providing a sense of immediate accomplishment. For instance, a short-term goal could be attending a social event or joining a local club or group where individuals can engage with like-minded individuals who share similar interests.

Long-term goals, on the other hand, can be focused on broader aspects of life. These might include pursuing education or vocational training, seeking employment opportunities, or even building deeper, more meaningful relationships. Breaking down long-term goals into smaller, manageable steps can make them appear less daunting and more attainable.

Remember, setting realistic goals does not mean compromising ambition. It simply ensures that the objectives are within reach, setting individuals up for success rather than disappointment. Celebrate each milestone achieved, no matter how small, as it signifies progress towards a more socially connected life.

OVERCOMING CHALLENGES: NAVIGATING THE PATH AHEAD

The journey towards reintegration is not without its challenges. It is crucial to anticipate and prepare for potential obstacles that may arise along the way. By doing so, individuals can develop strategies to overcome these challenges and sustain their progress.

One common challenge individuals face is a fear of judgment or rejection. After extended periods of isolation, the prospect of interacting with others can be daunting. It is important to recognize that everyone has unique experiences, and it is unlikely that others will fully understand one's journey. Embrace the idea that growth and change happen at different paces for everyone and do not let fear of judgment impede progress.

Developing a support system is vital when facing challenges. Connecting with individuals who have faced similar situations or experiences can provide valuable insights, empathy, and encouragement. Peer support groups or online communities can be powerful resources where individuals can share their struggles, learn from others, and offer support in return.

Equally important, practicing self-care throughout the reintegration process is crucial. Engaging in activities that promote physical and mental well-being, such as exercise, meditation, or pursuing hobbies and interests, can help individuals navigate the challenges they may encounter. Remember to be patient with oneself and acknowledge that setbacks are a normal part of the journey. Embrace these setbacks as opportunities for growth and learning, rather than as failures.

The path toward reintegration into society requires dedication, resilience, and a willingness to step outside of one's comfort zone. By focusing on skill-building, setting realistic goals, and overcoming challenges, individuals can gradually transform their lives and forge meaningful connections. In the second half of this chapter, we will explore additional strategies and insights that will further empower individuals on their journey towards social integration.

Stay tuned for the next part, where we delve into the importance of self-reflection and the role of empathy in reintegration. In the second half of this chapter, we will delve deeper into two essential components of the reintegration process: self-reflection and empathy. These elements play a crucial role in helping individuals build stronger connections and foster a sense of belonging in society.

SELF-REFLECTION: UNDERSTANDING
YOUR JOURNEY

Before diving into the process of reintegration, it is important to take the time for self-reflection. This introspective practice allows individuals to better understand their experiences, strengths, and areas for growth. By gaining a deeper awareness of oneself, individuals can navigate the reintegration process with more clarity and purpose.

Start by taking inventory of your strengths and achievements. Reflect on past experiences where you have successfully overcome challenges or taken steps towards social connection. Celebrate these milestones as they are evidence of your resilience and ability to grow. Acknowledging your strengths can boost confidence and remind you of your inner resources.

Next, consider any patterns or habits that hindered social integration in the past. Was it fear of judgment or rejection? Difficulty initiating conversations? Reflecting on these challenges can help identify areas where you may need to focus your efforts. Remember, self-reflection is a tool for learning and growth – it is not an opportunity for self-criticism or judgment. Be compassionate with yourself as you explore these areas.

Another valuable technique in self-reflection is journaling. By putting your thoughts and experiences on paper, you can gain new insights and perspectives. Use your journal as a safe space to express your emotions and reflect on your progress. Consider writing about your goals, setbacks, and any lessons learned along the way. This practice can be immensely helpful in developing self-awareness and promoting personal growth.

Empathy: Cultivating Connection with Others

Empathy plays a crucial role in fostering meaningful connections and building relationships. It is the ability to understand and share the feelings of others, which helps create a sense of understanding and compassion.

To cultivate empathy, start by practicing active listening. When engaging in conversations, make a conscious effort to be fully present. Focus on the speaker's words, body language, and emotions. By giving others your undivided attention, you demonstrate respect and create a safe space for open communication.

Additionally, empathy can be nurtured through perspective-taking. Put yourself in someone else's shoes and try to understand their experiences, challenges, and emotions. This exercise helps develop a deeper sense of empathy and compassion towards others. It allows you to approach interactions with an open mind and a willingness to understand different perspectives. Building empathy also involves practicing kindness and compassion towards oneself. It is essential to treat yourself with the same understanding and care that you extend to others. Remember that everyone makes mistakes, and setbacks are a natural part of the journey. Embrace self-compassion as a means to bounce back from challenges and continue moving forward.

In addition to self-reflection and empathy, it is crucial to continue seeking support throughout the reintegration process. Utilize the resources available to you, such as therapists, counselors, and support groups. These individuals and communities can provide guidance, validation, and encouragement as you navigate the complexities of reconnecting with society.

As you progress on your journey towards reintegration, remember that each person's path is unique. Comparing your progress to others' is not productive and can hinder your growth. Focus on your own progress, celebrate your achievements, and remain patient with yourself throughout the process.

In conclusion, the process of reintegration requires an

ongoing commitment to self-reflection, empathy, and personal growth. By understanding your own journey, cultivating empathy for others, and seeking support, you can forge meaningful connections and reintegrate into society. Remember, this is a transformative journey, and the rewards are well worth the effort.

With the second half of this chapter complete, we have explored the importance of self-reflection and empathy in the reintegration process. These concepts serve as powerful tools to deepen self-awareness, foster compassion, and build connections with others. In the next chapter, we will delve into the topic of resilience and explore strategies to overcome setbacks and persist in the face of challenges. Stay tuned as we continue this enlightening exploration of hikikomori, understanding, and overcoming social isolation.

CHAPTER 9: EMPATHY AND UNDERSTANDING

Social isolation is a complex phenomenon that affects individuals worldwide, with hikikomori being a prominent manifestation of this issue. These individuals withdraw from social interactions and isolate themselves from society, often spending vast amounts of time confined to their homes or rooms. Hikikomori is not simply a choice or a phase; rather, it is a deeply rooted psychological, emotional, and societal problem that requires our empathetic understanding and support.

In order to truly comprehend the experiences of those suffering from hikikomori, it is essential for us to delve into the underlying causes. Various factors contribute to the development of this condition, such as societal pressures, academic stress, bullying, and family dysfunction. These individuals feel overwhelmed by the expectations and demands of the world around them, leading them to adopt a self-imposed isolation as a coping mechanism. It is crucial for society to recognize that hikikomori is not a result of laziness or apathy but a response to deep-seated distress.

Empathy plays a vital role in addressing hikikomori and facilitating the recovery process. By putting ourselves in the shoes of those experiencing social isolation, we can begin to comprehend the profound loneliness and despair they endure. It is through empathy that we can break down the barriers of judgment and stigma towards hikikomori, fostering a greater sense of understanding and acceptance within society.

One significant step towards cultivating empathy is to acknowledge the impact of societal expectations on individuals. Our society often prioritizes achievement, productivity, and conformity, which places immense pressure on individuals, particularly the youth. By recognizing and challenging these societal norms, we can create an environment that is more compassionate and inclusive, allowing those struggling with hikikomori to feel accepted and understood.

Education is another key component in fostering empathy towards hikikomori. By providing accurate information about this condition, we can dispel common misconceptions and myths surrounding it. Schools, universities, and communities should introduce educational initiatives that teach students and the general public about the realities of hikikomori, its potential causes, and the impact it has on individuals and families. By educating ourselves and others, we can help reduce misunderstanding and prejudice, promoting a more empathetic society.

Simultaneously, it is essential to establish support systems that offer a compassionate approach towards individuals experiencing hikikomori. Mental health professionals, social workers, and counselors should receive appropriate training to effectively address the unique needs of those struggling with this condition. Additionally, helplines and support groups can provide individuals with a safe and non-judgmental space to express their feelings, fears, and concerns. Developing these resources ensures that individuals experiencing hikikomori can access the help they need and find encouragement to gradually reintegrate into society.

Beyond individual efforts, it is crucial for society as a whole to adopt a compassionate and empathetic approach. Stereotypes and stigmatization only serve to worsen the isolation and distress faced by hikikomori individuals. Instead, by nurturing an environment that encourages open dialogue, understanding, and support, we can facilitate their recovery and prevent social isolation from becoming a lifelong struggle.

As we continue to explore the significance of empathy and understanding towards hikikomori, we realize the imperative nature of changing our perspectives and attitudes. Each of us has the power to contribute to a society that stands against judgment and embraces compassion. By doing so, we pave the way for a more inclusive and empathetic world, where hikikomori individuals can find solace, understanding, and the opportunity to reintegrate into society.

In the second half of this chapter, we will delve deeper into the role of empathy and understanding in supporting individuals experiencing hikikomori. By examining specific strategies and initiatives, we can gain a better understanding of how society can actively contribute to reducing social isolation and aiding in the recovery process.

One crucial aspect of fostering empathy and understanding towards hikikomori individuals is promoting open dialogue and reducing the stigma associated with this condition. Open discussions can help break down the barriers of judgment and encourage greater acceptance within society. Creating safe spaces where hikikomori individuals can share their stories and experiences without fear of ridicule or condemnation is vital. Support groups, online forums, or community organizations can provide these spaces, allowing individuals to connect with others who have gone through similar struggles. These platforms not only offer validation and support but also facilitate the exchange of coping mechanisms and strategies for overcoming social isolation.

Moreover, it is essential to empower hikikomori individuals by involving them directly in initiatives aimed at improving their situation. Ensuring that they have a voice in decision-making processes allows for more comprehensive and empathetic solutions. By actively engaging with hikikomori individuals and including their perspectives in the development of support services, we can address their specific needs and concerns more effectively.

Another crucial aspect of empathy towards hikikomori individuals is understanding the potential long-term consequences of social isolation. It is important to recognize that the longer individuals experience hikikomori, the harder it becomes for them to reconnect with society. This understanding should motivate us to take early intervention seriously, implementing preventive measures and support systems in schools, communities, and families.

Schools, in particular, play a significant role in nurturing empathy and understanding towards hikikomori individuals. Teachers and educators should receive training on recognizing the signs of social isolation and understanding the underlying causes. By fostering a supportive and inclusive learning environment and promoting mental health education, schools can contribute to the prevention and early intervention of hikikomori.

Additionally, family dynamics can significantly influence an individual's vulnerability to hikikomori. It is crucial for families to possess an awareness and understanding of this condition, allowing them to offer the necessary support and assistance. Family therapy and counseling can provide a platform for open dialogue, helping families navigate the challenges associated with hikikomori and strengthening familial relationships.

Mental health professionals also play a key role in developing empathy and understanding towards hikikomori individuals. It is essential for these professionals to undergo training that focuses on the unique needs and experiences of those struggling with social isolation. By equipping them with the knowledge and skills required, we can ensure hikikomori individuals receive appropriate and empathetic care.

In order to provide comprehensive support, a multidisciplinary approach is crucial. Collaboration between mental health professionals, educators, social workers, and community organizations is necessary to address the multifaceted challenges faced by hikikomori individuals. This collaboration allows for a holistic understanding of the individual's circumstances, enabling more effective and tailored interventions.

Furthermore, it is important to acknowledge that recovery is a gradual and individualized process for hikikomori individuals. The road to reintegration into society may be daunting and filled with setbacks. Patience, support, and understanding from society are crucial during this journey. By reframing our expectations and celebrating each step towards reengagement, we can ensure an environment that promotes resilience and success.

Society as a whole must recognize the immense value of empathy and understanding towards hikikomori individuals. By demonstrating compassion and actively challenging the stigmatization surrounding social isolation, we can create a culture of acceptance and support. By doing so, we foster an environment where those experiencing hikikomori can find hope, understanding, and the opportunity to rebuild their lives.

In conclusion, empathy and understanding are fundamental in addressing the complex phenomenon of hikikomori. By emphasizing the significance of empathy and implementing concrete strategies, we can facilitate the recovery process, reduce social isolation, and create a more inclusive society. Through open dialogue, supportive environments, and multidisciplinary approaches, we can ensure that hikikomori individuals have access to the resources, understanding, and acceptance necessary to reintegrate into society. Let us stand together to conquer social isolation and build a brighter future for all individuals affected by hikikomori.

CHAPTER 10: ENHANCING SOCIAL SKILLS AND COMMUNICATION

In a world that thrives on connections and interpersonal relationships, social isolation poses numerous challenges. The world of Hikikomori, a term coined in Japan to describe individuals who withdraw from society, demands our attention. In this chapter, we delve into strategies for understanding and overcoming social isolation, with a focus on enhancing social skills and communication.

Developing essential social skills is crucial for individuals facing social isolation. These skills lay the foundation for healthy interactions, enabling individuals to navigate the complexities of social relationships. By recognizing the importance of social skills development, we pave the way for successful reintegration into society.

To begin, let us explore a fundamental social skill: active listening. Active listening involves giving one's full attention to the speaker, demonstrating interest and empathy. By being present in conversations, we not only show respect for others but also foster deeper connections. Practice active listening by focusing on the speaker's words, maintaining eye contact, and offering appropriate non-verbal cues, such as nodding or smiling. These small actions can have a profound impact, making the speaker feel heard and valued.

Alongside active listening, effective communication skills are essential. Clear and concise communication enables individuals to express their thoughts, emotions, and needs effectively. However, social isolation often hampers the development of these skills. To overcome this challenge, it is beneficial to engage in activities that promote communication, such as joining support groups or participating in workshops specifically designed to enhance communication abilities. Through these platforms, individuals can gradually regain their confidence in expressing themselves and gradually improve their communication skills.

Another valuable technique for enhancing social skills is the practice of mindfulness. Mindfulness cultivates self-awareness and allows individuals to observe their thoughts, feelings, and actions without judgment. By developing mindfulness, one can become more attuned to social cues, empathize with others, and regulate their own emotions. Incorporating mindfulness exercises, such as meditation or deep breathing, into daily routines can lay the groundwork for self-growth and improved social interactions.

While focusing on individual social skills development is crucial, the creation of a supportive network is equally important. Fostering connections with others who share similar experiences can provide a sense of belonging and understanding. Support groups, whether physical or virtual, offer a safe space for individuals to discuss their challenges, share insights, and receive encouragement. Surrounding oneself with a supportive community can inspire hope and provide guidance during the journey of overcoming social isolation.

Furthermore, relationships with family and friends play a pivotal role in a successful reintegration process. Loved ones can offer valuable support, understanding, and motivation. For family members and friends, educating themselves about social isolation and its impact is vital. By seeking knowledge and understanding, they can play an active role in the recovery process, providing the necessary encouragement and support.

In summary, enhancing social skills and communication is a multifaceted endeavor that requires dedication and perseverance. Through active listening, effective communication, mindfulness, and the cultivation of supportive connections, individuals facing social isolation can reclaim their place in society. By implementing these strategies, one begins the transformation from a state of isolation to a fulfilling life filled with meaningful social interactions.

As we delve deeper into the strategies for overcoming social isolation and understanding the complexities of reintegration, the second half of this chapter promises to explore additional tools and techniques. Stay tuned for an in-depth exploration of interventions, strategies for building assertiveness, and successful long-term integration into society. The journey towards rebuilding lives is ongoing, but with continued support and effort, individuals facing social isolation can find hope, connection, and a fulfilling life beyond their seclusion.

As we continue our exploration of enhancing social skills and communication, we will delve into additional tools and techniques that can aid in the journey of overcoming social isolation and achieving successful reintegration. In this second half of the chapter, we will discuss interventions, strategies for building assertiveness, and fostering long-term integration into society.

Interventions play a crucial role in supporting individuals facing social isolation. These interventions can take various forms, ranging from therapeutic approaches to structured programs designed to address specific social skill deficits. Cognitive-behavioral therapy (CBT) is one such intervention that has shown promising results in helping individuals overcome social isolation. CBT focuses on identifying negative thought patterns and replacing them with more constructive and optimistic ones. Through CBT, individuals can develop a more positive self-image and improve their ability to navigate social interactions.

Another effective intervention technique is social skills training. This type of training provides individuals with the opportunity to learn and practice social skills in a safe and supportive environment. Role-playing exercises, group discussions, and simulated social scenarios are often utilized to build confidence and enhance communication abilities. By engaging in these training sessions, individuals can gain valuable feedback, learn from their experiences, and gradually improve their social skills over time.

Building assertiveness is a crucial aspect of enhancing social skills and communication. Often, individuals facing social isolation may struggle with low self-esteem or assertiveness issues, resulting in difficulties in expressing their wants, needs, and boundaries effectively. To address this, it is important to develop assertiveness skills, which involve being able to confidently and respectfully communicate one's thoughts, feelings, and preferences.

One effective strategy for building assertiveness is practicing assertive communication. This involves expressing oneself clearly and directly, while also considering the feelings and perspectives of others. By using "I" statements, individuals can express their thoughts and emotions without placing blame or causing defensiveness. Additionally, setting boundaries and learning to say "no" when necessary are essential aspects of assertiveness. Through consistent practice and reinforcement, individuals can gradually develop their assertiveness skills and improve their ability to navigate social interactions successfully.

To foster long-term integration into society, it is vital to embrace a growth mindset and be open to continuous learning and self-improvement. Recognizing that social skills take time and effort to develop is essential, as it allows individuals to approach their journey with patience and perseverance. It is also crucial to maintain a positive outlook and celebrate small successes along the way, as this can provide motivation and reinforce progress.

As individuals continue to work on enhancing their social skills and communication, it is important for them to actively seek opportunities for social engagement. Joining clubs, organizations, or community activities that align with one's interests allows for the cultivation of new relationships and the practice of newly acquired social skills. Volunteering is another excellent way to connect with others and develop a sense of purpose and belonging.

Additionally, embracing technology can be a valuable tool for individuals facing social isolation. Online communities, forums, and social media platforms provide opportunities for connection and interaction, allowing individuals to bridge the geographical and social gaps that may exist in their lives. Virtual support groups and webinars focusing on social skill development and overcoming social isolation can also be beneficial.

Throughout the process of enhancing social skills and communication, it is important to remember that setbacks are a natural part of any journey. The road to successful reintegration may not always be smooth, and individuals may face moments of discomfort, self-doubt, or anxiety. During these times, it is crucial to practice self-compassion and resilience. Being kind to oneself, seeking support from trusted individuals, and remaining committed to personal growth can help individuals navigate through difficult moments and continue on their path towards integration and fulfillment.

In conclusion, enhancing social skills and communication is a multifaceted endeavor that requires dedication, practice, and continuous learning. Through interventions, assertiveness-building strategies, and a growth mindset, individuals facing social isolation can gradually overcome their challenges and reintegrate into society. By embracing opportunities for social engagement, leveraging technology, and practicing self-compassion, individuals can find hope, connection, and a fulfilling life beyond their previous isolation.

CHAPTER 11: MANAGING ANXIETY AND DEPRESSION

Anxiety and depression are common mental health challenges faced by individuals with Hikikomori experience. These conditions can greatly exacerbate the sense of isolation and hinder progress towards reintegration into society. In this chapter, we will delve into various strategies and coping mechanisms that can help manage anxiety and depression in the context of Hikikomori. By exploring these approaches, individuals can find ways to alleviate their symptoms and work towards a healthier and more fulfilling life.

Understanding Anxiety and Depression

Before we embark on discussing strategies to manage anxiety and depression, it is crucial to have a basic understanding of these conditions. Anxiety is a generalized feeling of unease, fear, or worry that can manifest in various forms such as panic attacks, social anxiety, or specific phobias. It can be a constant presence or occur in response to specific triggers. On the other hand, depression involves persistent feelings of sadness, hopelessness, and loss of interest or pleasure in activities. It affects one's emotions, thoughts, and overall well-being.

Building a Supportive Network

One vital aspect of managing anxiety and depression is to establish a supportive network. Isolation can intensify these mental health challenges, so reaching out to reliable and compassionate individuals can make a significant difference. Building relationships with understanding family members, close friends, or support groups can offer valuable emotional support and an opportunity to share experiences. Additionally, trained professionals such as psychologists or therapists can provide crucial guidance and therapy tailored to individual needs.

Engaging in Therapy

Therapy is an essential tool in managing anxiety and depression. Cognitive-behavioral therapy (CBT), for example, focuses on identifying and challenging negative thoughts and behavior patterns. Through CBT, individuals can develop effective coping mechanisms and gain a greater understanding of their triggers. Another therapeutic approach, known as mindfulness-based therapy, emphasizes living in the present moment and cultivating self-awareness. This can help individuals better recognize their emotions and manage them in a healthier manner.

Adopting Self-Care Techniques

Self-care practices greatly contribute to managing anxiety and depression. Engaging in activities that bring joy, relaxation, and a sense of accomplishment can have a positive impact on mental well-being. Regular exercise, for instance, has been shown to reduce symptoms of anxiety and depression by releasing endorphins, the brain's natural mood boosters. Additionally, practicing mindfulness and relaxation techniques, such as meditation or deep breathing exercises, can aid in calming an overwhelmed mind.

Developing Coping Mechanisms

It is crucial to explore and develop personal coping mechanisms to address anxiety and depression. Engaging in creative outlets, such as art, writing, or playing music, can serve as effective means of self-expression and stress relief. Expressing emotions through creative channels can help individuals process their thoughts and experience a sense of catharsis. Engaging in hobbies and activities that bring a sense of purpose and accomplishment can boost self-esteem and provide a distraction from negative thoughts.

Exploring Medication Options

In some cases, medication can be a valuable tool in managing anxiety and depression. Consultation with a psychiatrist or primary care physician can help individuals determine if medication is necessary and explore appropriate options. Medication should always be prescribed and monitored by professionals to ensure its effectiveness and minimize potential side effects. It is important to note that medication is not a standalone solution but can complement other therapeutic approaches.

In the first half of this chapter, we have discussed various strategies and coping mechanisms for managing anxiety and depression within the context of Hikikomori. Building a supportive network, engaging in therapy, adopting self-care techniques, developing personal coping mechanisms, and exploring medication options are crucial steps towards improving mental well-being. By implementing these approaches, individuals can begin their journey towards overcoming social isolation and reclaiming their lives.

Exploring Advanced Techniques and Additional Guidance

Now we move on to managing anxiety and depression within the context of Hikikomori, we will delve into more advanced techniques and provide additional guidance to help individuals effectively cope with these mental health challenges. By expanding our knowledge and implementing these strategies, individuals can take significant steps towards improving their overall well-being and combating social isolation.

Identifying Triggers and Developing Coping Strategies

To effectively manage anxiety and depression, it is crucial to identify and understand the triggers that contribute to these feelings. Each individual may have different triggers, and recognizing them can be a valuable tool in developing appropriate coping strategies. Keeping a journal or using a mood tracker can help to identify patterns and potential triggers. Once identified, individuals can then work on developing coping mechanisms that suit their needs.

One coping strategy is the use of grounding techniques. These techniques help individuals focus their attention on the present moment and can provide immediate relief during moments of anxiety or depression. Simple grounding exercises include deep breathing, counting objects in the room, touching textured surfaces, or using aromatherapy with calming scents. These techniques can help bring individuals back to the present and alleviate distressing thoughts and emotions.

Managing Negative Thoughts through Cognitive Restructuring

Negative thoughts and cognitive distortions can significantly impact anxiety and depression. Cognitive restructuring is a powerful technique that involves challenging and replacing negative thoughts with more realistic and positive ones. By reframing negative thinking patterns, individuals can change the way they perceive themselves and their circumstances.

One effective method for cognitive restructuring is the ABCDE model. This model involves identifying the activating event (A), recognizing the irrational belief or negative thought (B), analyzing the consequences (C), disputing the negative thought (D), and finally, energizing oneself with a more positive and rational belief (E). This systematic approach encourages individuals to challenge their negative thoughts and replace them with more realistic and positive interpretations.

Rebuilding Social Connections and Establishing Boundaries

As individuals strive towards overcoming social isolation, it is essential to rebuild social connections while also establishing and maintaining healthy boundaries. Participating in social activities can gradually reintegrate individuals into society and help alleviate feelings of loneliness. Joining support groups or engaging in volunteer work related to their interests can provide opportunities for social interaction and a sense of purpose.

However, it is equally important to establish boundaries that prioritize self-care and mental well-being. Learning to say no when feeling overwhelmed and setting clear limits on social interactions can prevent burnout and ensure individuals allocate enough time and energy to take care of themselves. Building a balanced and sustainable social life is key to managing anxiety and depression in the context of Hikikomori.

Utilizing Technology as a Supportive Tool

In today's digital age, technology can play a significant role in supporting individuals struggling with anxiety and depression. Online support communities and forums can serve as a valuable resource for individuals with limited social interaction opportunities. These platforms offer a space to connect with others, share experiences, and gain support from individuals who can relate to their challenges.

In addition to support communities, there are also various mental health apps and online resources available. These tools can provide guided meditations, self-help modules, mood tracking features, and cognitive behavioral therapy exercises. However, it is important to use these resources in conjunction with professional guidance and not rely solely on them for treatment.

Continued Professional Support and Reevaluation

Throughout the journey of managing anxiety and depression, continued professional support is essential. Therapists, psychologists, or psychiatrists can provide ongoing guidance, monitor progress, and make adjustments to treatment plans as needed. Regular check-ins with these professionals can help individuals track their progress, identify areas for improvement, and ensure that they are consistently supported in their journey towards recovery.

Moreover, it is crucial to regularly reevaluate and reassess the effectiveness of coping strategies and treatment plans. With the guidance of professionals, individuals can make necessary adjustments and explore new interventions that may better suit their needs as they progress towards overcoming anxiety and depression.

Conclusion

In this second half of Chapter 12, we have explored more advanced techniques and provided additional guidance to help individuals effectively manage anxiety and depression within the context of Hikikomori. By identifying triggers and developing coping strategies, challenging negative thoughts through cognitive restructuring, rebuilding social connections while establishing boundaries, utilizing technology as a supportive tool, and continuing professional support, individuals can take significant steps towards finding relief from anxiety and depression and reclaiming their lives.

Remember, recovery is a personal journey, and progress may vary for each individual. With determination, perseverance, and the right support, it is possible to overcome the challenges of social isolation and achieve mental well-being. In the next chapter, we will shift our focus to exploring the process of reintegration into society and the steps individuals can take towards reconnecting with their communities.

CHAPTER 12: EDUCATION AND EMPLOYMENT OPPORTUNITIES

Social isolation can have a profound impact on an individual's education and employment opportunities. For those who have experienced a period of hikikomori, reintegrating into society can sometimes feel overwhelming and daunting. However, by exploring various options and resources, we can discover pathways that lead to a brighter future.

Education plays a pivotal role in shaping one's life, providing not only knowledge but also an opportunity for personal growth and skill development. For individuals seeking to overcome social isolation, it is crucial to explore alternative educational methods that align with their specific needs and circumstances. Traditional classroom settings may be intimidating for those who have spent a significant amount of time in solitude. Therefore, considering online learning platforms, vocational courses, or even distance education can offer a more flexible and comfortable environment for individuals on their journey of reintegration.

Online learning has become increasingly popular in recent years, presenting various opportunities for individuals to obtain new knowledge and skills. Platforms such as Coursera, Udemy, and Khan Academy offer a vast array of courses in diverse fields, ranging from computer programming to creative writing or even specialized skills like graphic design or culinary arts. These platforms provide an accessible and affordable way to learn at one's own pace, enabling individuals to gain valuable qualifications and knowledge without the constraints of a traditional classroom setting.

Vocational courses are another avenue worth exploring for

those transitioning from hikikomori to a more engaged lifestyle. These courses focus on practical skills and can open doors to employment opportunities in specific industries. Examples include trade schools, where individuals can learn trades like plumbing, carpentry, or electrical work. Community colleges often offer vocational programs in fields such as healthcare, automotive technology, or computer science.

> These courses not only provide essential skills but also offer opportunities for networking and building connections within industries.

Distance education, particularly through accredited universities, provides another avenue of educational reintegration. Many universities now offer online degree programs that allow individuals to pursue higher education from the comfort of their own home. This approach allows for a sense of independence and flexibility as individuals balance their reintegration efforts with their own unique circumstances. Engaging part-time in distance education programs can be an effective way to regain confidence, boost self-esteem, and work towards long-term career goals.

> While education is a crucial aspect of overcoming social isolation, obtaining suitable employment is equally important for individuals seeking to reintegrate into society. Employment not only provides financial stability but also fosters a sense of purpose and belonging. However, re-entering the job market after a period of hikikomori may prove challenging for some individuals.

> One effective starting point in the search for employment is to utilize career development centers and job placement services. These organizations offer guidance in resume building, interview preparation, and job search strategies. They also provide valuable networking opportunities and connections that can help individuals find suitable employment opportunities. These services are especially beneficial for individuals who may have gaps in their employment history or who are unsure about how to present themselves to potential employers.

> Another option to consider is volunteering. Engaging in

volunteer work allows individuals to gain practical experience, develop new skills, and establish positive references. Volunteering not only enhances one's resume but also provides a sense of community engagement, boosting self-confidence and facilitating the transition back into the workforce.

Internships and apprenticeships provide yet another avenue for individuals seeking employment opportunities. These programs allow individuals to gain practical experience in a specific field while learning from professionals. Internships and apprenticeships can serve as stepping stones towards securing long-term employment, providing individuals with valuable on-the-job training and a chance to prove their capabilities.

As we delve deeper into exploring education and employment opportunities for individuals reintegrating after a period of hikikomori, it becomes evident that a range of possibilities exists. By stepping outside one's comfort zone and exploring alternative paths, individuals can find avenues that lead to personal growth, renewed purpose, and meaningful connections. In the second half of this chapter, we will further explore the importance of mentorship, peer support groups, and community involvement in the reintegration process. But for now, we have only begun to scratch the surface of the many options available. Everything lies ahead, waiting to be discovered.

Mentorship plays a significant role in the journey of reintegrating individuals after a period of hikikomori into society, providing guidance, support, and direction. Having a mentor can offer invaluable insights, encouragement, and a sense of accountability as individuals navigate their education and employment opportunities. By connecting with someone who has successfully overcome social isolation or experienced a similar journey, individuals can gain valuable lessons, learn from their experiences, and develop the necessary skills for their own reintegration process.

A mentor can provide personalized advice and guidance tailored to the specific needs and circumstances of the individual.

They can offer practical tips on how to approach challenges, set goals, and develop effective strategies for success. Mentors can also serve as a source of motivation, encouraging individuals to push past their comfort zones, take calculated risks, and embrace new opportunities.

Finding a mentor can be done through various avenues. Local community centers, support groups, or online platforms dedicated to hikikomori and social isolation are great places to start. These platforms often connect individuals who have successfully reintegrated into society with those who are currently going through the process. Engaging with these communities allows individuals to share experiences, gain support, and establish connections with potential mentors.

Peer support groups are another important aspect of the reintegration journey. Connecting with individuals who have gone through similar experiences can create a sense of belonging, understanding, and empathy. These groups offer a space where individuals can openly discuss their challenges, share strategies, and offer encouragement to one another.

Engaging with community organizations and local initiatives is also crucial in the reintegration process. Participating in activities that align with personal interests, such as joining clubs, attending workshops, or volunteering, can help individuals develop social skills, build confidence, and expand their network. These activities provide opportunities to meet like-minded individuals, forge new relationships, and explore potential career paths.

Additionally, community involvement can aid individuals in transitioning back into the workforce. Often, community organizations host job fairs, networking events, and workshops that specifically cater to individuals seeking employment opportunities. These events not only allow individuals to connect with potential employers but also provide resources and support tailored to their unique circumstances.

Building a strong support system is key to overcoming the challenges that come with reintegrating into society. Surrounding oneself with positive and supportive individuals who believe in their potential can greatly impact an individual's journey. Family and close friends can serve as a pillar of support, offering emotional encouragement, understanding, and practical assistance throughout the process.

Self-care and personal well-being should also be prioritized during the reintegration process. Practicing self-care activities, such as exercise, meditation, hobbies, and spending time in nature, can help individuals manage stress, improve mental well-being, and cultivate a healthy work-life balance. Taking care of one's physical and mental health is essential for long-term success and overall happiness.

In conclusion, education and employment opportunities are crucial aspects of the reintegration process after a period of hikikomori. By exploring alternative educational methods, such as online learning, vocational courses, and distance education, individuals can tailor their educational journey to their specific needs and circumstances. Similarly, utilizing career development centers, job placement services, and considering volunteering, internships, and apprenticeships can open doors to employment opportunities. Mentorship, peer support groups, and community involvement play significant roles in providing guidance, support, and opportunities for growth. By combining these strategies and embracing the possibilities that lie ahead, individuals can overcome social isolation, find renewed purpose, and establish meaningful connections as they reintegrate into society. The path to a brighter future awaits, and with determination and perseverance, the possibilities are endless.

CHAPTER 13: PREVENTING HIKIKOMORI IN YOUTH

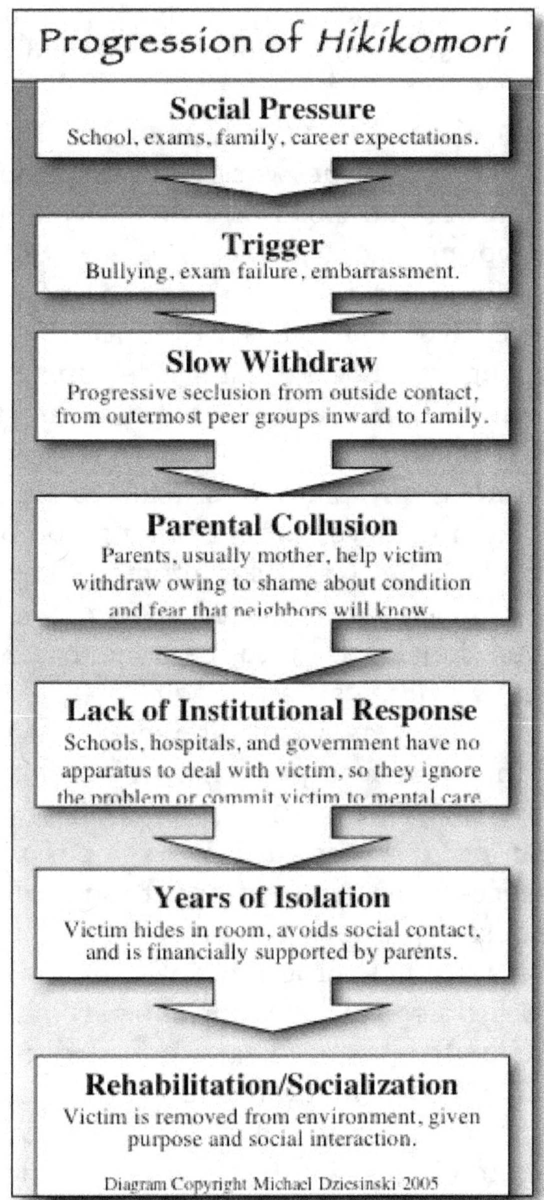

Addressing preventive approaches to reduce Hikikomori among youth, including early intervention, mental health awareness programs, and fostering positive peer relationships.

In recent years, the phenomenon of Hikikomori has garnered significant attention worldwide. Hikikomori refers to the social withdrawal and isolation experienced by individuals, predominantly young people, who choose to withdraw from society and confine themselves to their homes. This chapter focuses on preventive approaches to reduce the prevalence of Hikikomori among youth, addressing the importance of early intervention, mental health awareness programs, and fostering positive peer relationships.

Early intervention plays a crucial role in minimizing the risk of Hikikomori development among young individuals. Identifying the early signs and symptoms is key to providing the necessary support and resources. Parents, educators, and healthcare professionals need to be vigilant in recognizing signs of social withdrawal and isolation in youth. These signs may include avoiding social interactions, declining school attendance, changes in sleep patterns, and a lack of interest in previously enjoyed activities. By recognizing these warning signs, intervention can occur at the earliest stage possible, increasing the chances of successful reintegration into society.

One promising preventive measure is the implementation of mental health awareness programs in educational institutions. Incorporating psychological education as a part of the curriculum equips students with the necessary knowledge and skills to understand and address mental health challenges effectively. These programs can educate young individuals about the potential causes and impacts of Hikikomori, promoting empathy and encouraging them to seek help for themselves or their peers.

By normalizing mental health discussions and dismantling the stigma surrounding it, schools can play a vital role in preventing the onset of Hikikomori by fostering a supportive and inclusive environment.

Furthermore, fostering positive peer relationships is paramount in preventing Hikikomori among youth. Adolescence can be a challenging period, marked by social pressures and a desire to fit in. Creating opportunities for peer interaction and connection can reduce feelings of loneliness and isolation. Schools and community organizations can develop programs that facilitate social engagement, such as group activities, clubs, or mentorship initiatives. Encouraging collaboration and teamwork helps build social skills and enhances feelings of belonging, which are vital protective factors against Hikikomori development.

It is also essential to involve parents and caregivers in the preventive process. Parental support and understanding can significantly influence a young person's mental well-being. Encouraging open and honest communication with parents about mental health, providing them with resources and guidance, can help parents better recognize and respond to their child's emotional needs. Equipping parents with the tools to address potential stressors, such as academic pressure or social challenges, empowers them to play a proactive role in preventing Hikikomori.

In conclusion, preventing Hikikomori among youth requires a multi-faceted approach. Early intervention, mental health awareness programs, and fostering positive peer relationships are essential components in reducing the prevalence of this social issue. By identifying warning signs early on, integrating mental health education into schools, and promoting supportive peer networks, we can create a more inclusive society that raises awareness and understanding of Hikikomori. Developing comprehensive preventive measures will empower young individuals to navigate their challenges and foster a sense of connection and belonging in their lives.

To further prevent the development of hikikomori among youth, it is crucial to address societal factors that contribute to social isolation. While early intervention, mental health awareness programs, and positive peer relationships are fundamental preventive measures, addressing underlying issues will create a more inclusive environment for young individuals.

One key factor to consider is the influence of technology and social media on youth's mental health. With the rise of digital connectivity, young people are faced with immense pressure to constantly project a curated image of themselves. The fear of missing out (FOMO) and the pressure to conform to unrealistic standards can significantly impact their self-esteem and social interactions.

Therefore, incorporating digital resilience programs within educational institutions can be an effective preventive strategy. These programs aim to educate students about healthy online habits, critical thinking, and responsible use of social media. By teaching young individuals how to navigate the digital world effectively, they can better manage the negative effects of social media and reduce the risk of withdrawing from face-to-face interactions.

Additionally, it is essential to address the underlying causes of hikikomori, such as academic pressure and bullying. Education systems that emphasize academic achievements above all else can create an environment of intense competition and stress. This pressure can be overwhelming for some individuals, leading them to isolate themselves as a coping mechanism. By fostering holistic education that focuses on emotional well-being and personal growth, schools can alleviate academic pressure and create a more supportive atmosphere.

Furthermore, tackling bullying and promoting empathy within schools is crucial in preventing social isolation. Bullying can have severe psychological effects on its victims, often leading to feelings of shame, fear, and isolation. Schools should develop comprehensive anti-bullying programs that not only address the behavior itself but also promote understanding and empathy among students. By cultivating a culture of respect and acceptance, we can create a safer environment that discourages the development of hikikomori.

Involving mental health professionals in the preventive process is another vital aspect. Collaborating with psychologists, counselors, and therapists can provide an additional layer of support for young individuals. Schools and community organizations can partner with mental health professionals to offer counseling services or workshops on stress management, coping skills, and emotional well-being. By providing accessible mental health resources, we can ensure that young individuals receive the necessary support to prevent and address the early signs of hikikomori.

Moreover, it is essential to foster a sense of purpose and meaning in young individuals' lives. Many hikikomori individuals feel disconnected from society and lack motivation or a sense of direction. By offering career guidance, vocational training programs, or mentorship initiatives, we can help young people explore their interests, set goals, and develop a sense of purpose. Feeling a part of something bigger, whether it be through education, work, or community involvement, can significantly reduce the risk of social withdrawal and isolation.

In conclusion, preventing hikikomori in youth requires a comprehensive approach that addresses various factors contributing to social isolation. By incorporating digital resilience programs, combating academic pressure and bullying, involving mental health professionals, and fostering a sense of purpose, we can create a more inclusive society that supports the well-being of its young individuals. It is crucial for parents, educators, and community members to come together and prioritize the mental health and social connections of the youth. By implementing these preventive measures, we can pave the way for a brighter future, where hikikomori becomes a rare and manageable phenomenon.

CHAPTER 14: SUPPORTING HIKIKOMORI FOR PARENTS

On this chapter, we will delve into the crucial topic of supporting hikikomori parents. Parenting a child who is experiencing hikikomori can be an overwhelming and challenging experience. It often leaves parents feeling confused, helpless, and guilt-ridden. However, it is important to remember that parents play a vital role in helping their children overcome social isolation. By offering guidance, support, and coping strategies, parents can navigate the challenges they face and ultimately provide a strong foundation for their child's recovery. In this first half of the chapter, we will explore the initial steps parents can take to understand hikikomori and its impact on their child, as well as strategies for fostering open communication.

1. **Understanding Hikikomori:**

The first step for parents is to gain a deeper understanding of what hikikomori is and the effects it has on their child. Hikikomori refers to a condition experienced by individuals who withdraw from society, often confining themselves to their homes for an extended period of time. This social withdrawal can stem from various underlying factors, such as social anxiety, depression, or school-related stress.

Parents need to take the time to educate themselves about hikikomori, its causes, and the associated emotional and psychological struggles their child may be facing. By obtaining a comprehensive understanding of the condition, parents can better empathize with their child's experiences and provide appropriate support.

2. **Establishing Open Communication:**

Maintaining open lines of communication with their child is essential for parents supporting a hikikomori-affected individual. Reaching out to your child and demonstrating your willingness to listen without judgment can be challenging but crucial. Here are a few strategies to foster open communication:

a) Create a safe and non-judgmental space: Let your child know that they can express their thoughts, feelings, and concerns without fear of criticism or judgment. Creating a safe environment will encourage your child to open up about their struggles.

b) Active listening: Listen attentively when your child shares their experiences. Focus on understanding their emotions rather than offering immediate solutions. Validating their feelings helps create a sense of trust and empathy.

c) Ask open-ended questions: Instead of asking yes or no questions, pose open-ended questions that encourage your child to express themselves more fully. This approach allows them to explore their thoughts and feelings in-depth, fostering a deeper understanding between you both.

d) Be patient: Remember that building effective communication takes time. Your child may find it challenging to articulate their emotions. Encourage them without pressuring or overwhelming them. Patience is key to cultivating a sustainable and open dialogue.

3. Seeking Professional Support:

While parents are integral in their child's journey, seeking professional help is essential. Encourage your child to engage in therapy or counseling to access the specialized support they need. Therapists specializing in hikikomori can guide individuals towards recovery by addressing underlying issues, developing coping strategies, and rebuilding social skills.

As a parent, it is also crucial to seek support for yourself. Joining support groups or seeking counseling can provide a safe space for you to share your experiences, gain practical advice, and connect with others who are going through similar challenges. Remember, taking care of your own mental health equips you with the strength to support your child effectively.

Conclusion of the First Half:

In this first half of the chapter, we discussed the importance of understanding hikikomori and the impact it has on children. We explored strategies for fostering open communication, emphasizing the significance of creating a safe and non-judgmental space for your child. Additionally, we touched upon the necessity of seeking professional support for both your child and yourself as a parent. By following these initial steps, you lay the groundwork for a supportive and understanding relationship with your hikikomori-affected child.

SECOND HALF:

Encouraging Healthy Coping Mechanisms:

In addition to seeking professional support, it is crucial for parents to assist their hikikomori-affected child in developing healthy coping mechanisms. By doing so, parents can provide their child with effective tools to manage their emotions and navigate the challenges associated with social isolation. Here are some strategies to consider:

a) Encourage self-care: Help your child understand the importance of self-care and finding activities that promote well-being. Encourage them to engage in hobbies or interests that bring them joy and provide a sense of purpose.

b) Teach relaxation techniques: Introduce your child to relaxation techniques such as deep breathing exercises, meditation, or mindfulness. These practices can help reduce stress and anxiety, allowing for a calmer state of mind.

c) Promote physical activity: Encourage your child to engage in regular physical activity as it has been proven to have positive effects on mental health. Whether it's going for walks, practicing yoga, or participating in sports, physical exercise can improve mood and reduce feelings of isolation.

d) Foster healthy sleep habits: Encourage your child to establish a consistent sleep schedule and create a relaxing bedtime routine. Adequate sleep is essential for overall well-being and can contribute to improved mental health.

Setting Realistic Expectations:

It is crucial for parents to manage their own expectations

and accept that the recovery process for their hikikomori-affected child may take time. Setting unrealistic or pressured expectations can lead to feelings of failure or even exacerbate their child's anxiety. Here are some tips for setting realistic expectations:

a) Celebrate small victories: Recognize and celebrate any progress your child makes, no matter how small. Positive reinforcement can encourage motivation and boost their self-esteem.

b) Focus on the process, not just the outcome: Encourage your child to focus on the efforts they are making rather than solely on the final result. This approach helps them value their journey and understand that it's okay to encounter setbacks along the way.

c) Be patient and understanding: Understand that recovery is a gradual process and setbacks are a normal part of the journey. Avoid placing unnecessary pressure on your child, and instead provide encouragement and understanding.

d) Offer unconditional support: Assure your child that your love and support are unconditional. Let them know that you are there for them, no matter the challenges they face or the progress they make.

Creating a Supportive Network:

Building a supportive network of family, friends, and professionals can greatly benefit both the hikikomori-affected individual and their parents. This network can provide emotional support, practical advice, and reassurance that you are not alone in this journey. Consider the following steps:

a) Educate loved ones: Help your family and friends understand hikikomori and its effects by providing them with resources and information. This will enable them to offer empathetic support and minimize any potential judgment or misunderstanding.

b) Seek professional advice: Consult therapists or counselors who specialize in hikikomori to gain valuable insights and guidance. Their expertise can help you navigate your role as a parent, and they may also offer suggestions for support groups or other resources.

c) Join support groups: Consider joining support groups for parents of hikikomori-affected individuals. These groups create a safe space for sharing experiences, seeking advice, and connecting with others who are going through similar challenges. Remember, you are not alone in this journey.

d) Connect with other parents: Reach out to other parents who have faced or are currently facing similar situations. Their firsthand experiences and wisdom can offer valuable insights and practical strategies for supporting your child and yourself.

CONCLUSION:

In the second half of this chapter, we explored additional strategies for supporting hikikomori-affected individuals and their parents. We emphasized the importance of encouraging healthy coping mechanisms, setting realistic expectations, and creating a supportive network. By implementing these strategies, parents can continue to provide the necessary guidance, support, and understanding their child needs to overcome social isolation. Remember that every journey is unique, and it may take time, but with your unwavering support, your child can regain their confidence and ultimately lead a fulfilling life beyond hikikomori.

CHAPTER 15: OVERCOMING STIGMA AND BUILDING SELF-ESTEEM

Addressing the issue of stigma surrounding Hikikomori, focusing on self-acceptance, building self-esteem, and promoting a positive self-image in the journey towards recovery.

In the previous chapter, we explored the concept of Hikikomori and delved into the complexities of this social phenomenon. We discussed the various causes, symptoms, and the impact it has on individuals' lives. Now, as we move forward on our journey towards understanding and overcoming social isolation, we turn our attention to one of the biggest challenges faced by Hikikomori individuals - the stigma associated with this condition.

Understanding Stigma

Stigma can be defined as a negative perception or belief held by society towards a particular group or condition. In the case of Hikikomori, stigma is rooted in misconceptions, stereotypes, and a lack of awareness. This stigma often leads to further isolation and a profound sense of shame and guilt, hindering individuals from seeking help and impeding their progress towards recovery.

The Impact of Stigma

The impact of stigma on Hikikomori individuals cannot be understated. It exacerbates their feelings of loneliness, worthlessness, and self-doubt. Stigmatizing attitudes from family, friends, and society at large only serve to deepen their isolation, making it even more challenging to break free from their self-imposed seclusion. Consequently, building self-esteem and promoting self-acceptance becomes a crucial aspect of their recovery journey.

Promoting Self-Acceptance

One of the first steps towards overcoming stigma is cultivating self-acceptance. Hikikomori individuals often internalize society's negative perception of them, causing immense self-disapproval. To counteract this, it is essential for them to embrace self-acceptance and recognize that their worth and value as human beings are not defined solely by their condition.

Self-acceptance involves acknowledging their struggles, vulnerabilities, and past mistakes without judgment. It requires them to be compassionate towards themselves, understanding that everyone faces challenges throughout life. By fostering self-acceptance, Hikikomori individuals can begin to reframe their perceptions of themselves and develop a more positive self-image.

Building Self-Esteem

Building self-esteem is another crucial aspect of overcoming stigma and breaking free from the confines of Hikikomori. Low self-esteem often plagues individuals who have experienced prolonged social isolation, as they may doubt their abilities, feel incompetent, and question their worthiness of connection and acceptance.

To cultivate self-esteem, Hikikomori individuals need to focus on their strengths, talents, and accomplishments. Identifying their unique qualities and recognizing their achievements, no matter how small, can help foster a sense of pride and confidence. By setting achievable goals and working towards them, they can gradually rebuild their self-esteem and regain a sense of purpose in life.

Promoting a Positive Self-Image

Creating a positive self-image is integral to the recovery process. Hikikomori individuals often perceive themselves through the lens of societal stigma, which can be highly detrimental to their well-being. To counteract this, it is crucial to encourage a shift in their self-perception and help them construct a positive narrative about themselves.

Promoting a positive self-image involves reframing negative thoughts and beliefs into more empowering and supportive ones. Encouraging self-affirmations, reflective journaling, and engaging in activities that bring them joy and a sense of accomplishment can greatly contribute to the development of a positive self-image. Engaging in therapy or support groups can also provide them with a safe space to challenge their negative self-perception and gain valuable insights from others experiencing similar struggles.

Conclusion

In this first half of the chapter, we explored the detrimental effects of stigma on Hikikomori individuals. We emphasized the importance of self-acceptance, building self-esteem, and promoting a positive self-image as vital steps towards overcoming societal judgments. By cultivating self-acceptance, recognizing their strengths, and fostering a positive narrative, individuals on the Hikikomori recovery journey can empower themselves to break free from the confines of stigma. As we delve deeper into the second half of this chapter, we will explore practical strategies and tools that can aid individuals in overcoming stigma and building strong self-esteem. Methods to Overcome Stigma and Build Self-Esteem

In the first half of this chapter, we discussed the impact of stigma on Hikikomori individuals and highlighted the importance of self-acceptance, building self-esteem, and promoting a positive self-image as essential steps towards overcoming societal judgments. Now, in the second half of this chapter, we will explore practical strategies and tools that can aid individuals in overcoming stigma and building strong self-esteem.

Seeking Professional Support:

One of the most valuable resources on the journey towards overcoming stigma and building self-esteem is professional help. Therapists, counselors, and support groups specialized in Hikikomori recovery can provide a safe and non-judgmental environment in which individuals can express their emotions and explore their thoughts. These professionals can guide them through the process of recognizing and challenging negative self-perceptions, allowing for personal growth and development.

Mindfulness and Self-Reflection:

Practicing mindfulness can greatly contribute to overcoming stigma and building self-esteem. Mindfulness involves being present in the moment and observing thoughts, emotions, and physical sensations without judgment. By cultivating self-awareness through practices such as meditation and deep breathing exercises, individuals can become more attuned to their inner experiences and recognize when stigmatizing thoughts or beliefs arise. This increased awareness allows for the opportunity to challenge and reframe those thoughts, leading to a more positive self-perception.

Self-reflection is another powerful tool in the journey towards overcoming stigma and building self-esteem. Engaging in self-reflection involves setting aside time to reflect on one's experiences, emotions, and beliefs. By exploring the underlying reasons behind negative self-perception and identifying patterns of stigmatizing thoughts, individuals can begin to understand the origins of their low self-esteem and challenge those ingrained beliefs. Self-reflection also enables individuals to celebrate their progress, recognize their strengths, and acknowledge their efforts along the road to recovery.

Positive Affirmations:

Positive affirmations are constructive statements aimed at challenging negative self-perception and fostering a positive self-image. By repeating affirmations such as "I am worthy," "I am capable," or "I deserve love and acceptance," individuals can counteract the damaging effects of stigma and promote self-acceptance. Writing affirmations on sticky notes and placing them in visible areas can serve as reminders of their worth and potential, providing a constant source of support and encouragement.

Engaging in Meaningful Activities:

Engaging in activities that bring joy, fulfillment, and a sense of accomplishment can significantly contribute to building self-esteem and promoting a positive self-image. Hikikomori individuals can explore their hobbies and interests, engage in creative outlets such as painting, writing, or playing a musical instrument, or volunteer for a cause they believe in. By dedicating time to activities that align with their passions and aspirations, individuals can regain a sense of purpose, build self-confidence, and redefine their identity beyond the confines of their condition.

Cultivating Healthy Connections:

Connecting with others who have experienced or understand the challenges of Hikikomori can be immensely valuable in overcoming stigma and building self-esteem. Support groups, both online and in-person, provide opportunities to share experiences, gain insights, and receive support from individuals who have walked a similar path. Through these connections, individuals can dispel feelings of isolation, find validation, and build a supportive network of individuals who truly understand their journey.

Additionally, cultivating healthy connections with friends, family, or mentors who are accepting and understanding of their condition is crucial for building self-esteem. Surrounding oneself with positive influences promotes a sense of belonging and encourages individuals to appreciate their strengths and accomplishments.

Conclusion

In this second half of the chapter, we explored practical strategies and tools that can aid individuals in overcoming stigma and building self-esteem. Seeking professional support, practicing mindfulness and self-reflection, using positive affirmations, engaging in meaningful activities, and cultivating healthy connections are all important steps on the journey towards self-acceptance and personal growth.

Overcoming stigma and building self-esteem is not an overnight process; it requires dedication, patience, and the willingness to challenge deeply ingrained beliefs. However, with consistent effort and the support of others, Hikikomori individuals can empower themselves to break free from the confines of stigma and embark on a path towards recovery, connection, and a renewed sense of self.

CHAPTER 17: CULTURAL PERSPECTIVES ON SOCIAL ISOLATION

Social isolation, a phenomenon that transcends geographical borders, is experienced by individuals across different cultures and societies. While its prevalence and underlying causes may vary, examining how different cultures perceive and approach social isolation can shed light on diverse perspectives and foster a more comprehensive understanding. Through an exploration of various cultural perspectives, this chapter aims to unravel the nuances surrounding social isolation and highlight the potential solutions that can be derived from such insights.

In Japan, a country known for its high incidence of social isolation, the term "Hikikomori" has gained significant attention. Hikikomori refers to a state of extreme seclusion, where individuals voluntarily withdraw from society, often confining themselves in their homes for extended periods. This phenomenon has been a subject of great concern in Japanese society, prompting extensive research and cultural introspection. In Japan, social isolation is intertwined with societal pressures, such as academic or workplace performance, intense competition, and cultural norms that prioritize conformity.

The Japanese perspective on social isolation encompasses a balance between the desire for autonomy and the pressure to conform, leading to Hikikomori as a coping mechanism for some individuals.

Moving towards South Korea, another society grappling with social isolation, the concept of "Gyeo-hon Jel" sheds light on their cultural understanding. Translated as "overshadowed men," Gyeo-hon Jel refers to the social withdrawal experienced by

Korean men, particularly in their 30s and 40s, due to societal pressures and expectations.

This phenomenon, often attributed to economic factors, limited career prospects, and strain caused by high competition within education and employment, has far-reaching implications for mental health and wellbeing in Korean society. The perception of social isolation in South Korea emphasizes the significance of societal expectations and the subsequent impact on individuals' sense of self-worth and belonging.

In contrast, Indigenous cultures, such as those found among Native American communities in the United States, offer an alternative perspective on social isolation. These communities often prioritize communal living and emphasize interconnectedness, valuing the collective well-being above individual achievements. However, historical trauma, systemic marginalization, and the erosion of cultural practices have led to elevated rates of social isolation within Native American communities. Recognizing the cultural repercussions of colonization and intergenerational trauma is vital when exploring social isolation through the lens of Indigenous cultures. Promoting cultural revitalization initiatives and fostering a sense of community solidarity are essential components in addressing social isolation within these communities.

Turning our attention to Scandinavian countries, such as Norway and Finland, cultural perspectives on social isolation reveal a different societal approach. The concept of "Sisu" prevalent in these cultures emphasizes resilience, perseverance, and self-determination. This strength of character often contributes to a sense of community belonging and reduced social isolation. Furthermore, the promotion of social welfare policies and a strong welfare state in Scandinavian societies establishes a support system that mitigates feelings of isolation and fosters social cohesion. Cultural values in these countries emphasize interdependence, egalitarianism, and collective responsibility, underscoring the role of societal structures in addressing social isolation.

Each cultural perspective presented in this chapter offers valuable insights into the understanding and approach to social isolation. By examining diverse cultural contexts, we gain a deeper understanding of how social, historical, and economic factors intertwine to shape our perceptions of social isolation. Understanding the nuanced perspectives derived from cultural diversity can inform comprehensive strategies to combat social isolation effectively.

Continuing on from the diverse cultural perspectives on social isolation explored in the first half of this chapter, we now turn our attention to additional perspectives that offer valuable insights and understanding. These perspectives showcase how varying cultural contexts intersect with complex social dynamics, shedding light on different approaches and solutions to combat social isolation.

In China, the concept of Guānxì, which translates to "social connections" or "interpersonal relationships," holds great significance in the country's cultural landscape. Guānxì emphasizes the importance of networks and personal connections in various aspects of life, including business, politics, and social interactions. While this cultural value promotes social cohesion and communal support, it can also contribute to social isolation for individuals who lack strong Guānxì networks or struggle to navigate complex social hierarchies. The pressure to maintain and nurture these connections can be exhausting, leading some individuals to withdraw or isolate themselves socially. Thus, understanding the role of Guānxì in shaping social isolation in China requires an exploration of the delicate balance between the benefits and challenges associated with this cultural value.

Moving to **Brazil**, a country known for its vibrant and highly social culture, the concept of "saudade" offers a unique perspective on social isolation. Saudade is a Portuguese word that encapsulates feelings of longing, nostalgia, and a deep emotional connection to something or someone absent. While it may seem contradictory to associate this concept with social isolation, saudade reflects the deep-rooted sense of community and belonging that Brazilians hold dear. Nevertheless, in a rapidly changing society and urbanization, some individuals may experience social isolation due to the loss of traditional community structures and the erosion of interpersonal relationships. By acknowledging and understanding how cultural values such as saudade intersect with societal shifts, interventions can be formulated to tackle social isolation effectively.

Turning our focus to **sub-Saharan Africa**, where rich cultural diversity manifests in a range of perspectives on social isolation, the communal approach prevalent in many African societies offers important insights. In several African cultures, community and extended family networks play a central role in providing support and nurturing social connections. The Ubuntu philosophy, for example, emphasizes the interconnectedness of all individuals and promotes collective responsibility for the well-being of the community. However, rapid urbanization and economic disparities have led to the erosion of traditional social structures, contributing to a rise in social isolation in certain areas. Recognizing the resilience and strength of community ties, while also addressing the challenges posed by urbanization and modernization, is crucial in combating social isolation within African societies.

In India, a country characterized by its diversity, the concept of "Purdah" sheds light on a specific form of social isolation experienced by women. Purdah refers to the traditional practice of secluding women from public spaces and interactions with men outside their families. While the motivations behind Purdah vary and are intertwined with cultural, religious, and historical factors, it is crucial to recognize the potential for social isolation resulting from this practice. Efforts to address social isolation among women in Indian society must be sensitive to cultural diversity and engage in constructive dialogue to challenge gender norms, while also preserving cultural traditions and values.

As we broaden our understanding of social isolation through cultural perspectives, it becomes evident that diverse approaches are needed to address the complex interplay of social, historical, and economic factors. A comprehensive strategy should consider the unique cultural context of each society, valuing the strengths and challenges associated with their perspectives. By recognizing and respecting these cultural nuances, we can cultivate inclusive interventions and support systems tailored to specific communities, fostering a more connected and less isolated world.

In conclusion, this chapter has presented a range of cultural perspectives on social isolation, exploring how different societies perceive and approach this complex phenomenon. From Japan's Hikikomori to South Korea's Gyeo-hon Jel, and from Native American communities to Scandinavian countries, each perspective offers valuable insights into the impact of cultural values, societal structures, and historical legacies on social isolation. By embracing cultural diversity and understanding how nuanced perspectives shape our understanding, we can develop more effective strategies to combat social isolation and promote well-being and belonging for individuals across the globe.

CHAPTER 16: THE ROLE OF TECHNOLOGY AND SOCIAL MEDIA

In today's digital age, technology and social media have dramatically transformed the way we interact and communicate with each other. As we delve deeper into the understanding of hikikomori, it becomes crucial to explore how these technological advancements play a pivotal role in shaping and influencing hikikomori behavior. This chapter will examine the connection between hikikomori and technology, shedding light on the potential benefits, risks, and strategies for fostering a healthy online presence.

The Attraction of Technology:

One cannot underestimate the allure of technology for individuals experiencing hikikomori. Often, the virtual world provides a sense of solace, where social interactions can be controlled, and the pressures of face-to-face encounters can be avoided. Online platforms offer an escape from the overwhelming sensations and anxiety that can accompany real-world interactions. As a result, individuals with hikikomori tendencies may find themselves gravitating towards technology as a means of self-preservation and a refuge from the outside world.

However, it is crucial to acknowledge that technology's appeal goes beyond providing temporary relief. In a highly connected virtual landscape, individuals with hikikomori tendencies find communities and companionship that might otherwise be elusive offline. Online forums, specialized social media groups, and gaming communities serve as safe spaces for individuals to express themselves, connect with like-minded individuals, and form relationships, albeit in a digital context. The sense of belonging and understanding offered by these virtual communities can be powerful and profoundly impactful for those experiencing hikikomori.

The Potential Risks:

While technology undoubtedly presents opportunities for connectivity and support, it also poses potential risks for individuals with hikikomori tendencies. One of the primary concerns is the reinforcing of isolation through excessive technology use. The comfort and safety provided by the virtual world can inadvertently perpetuate and intensify hikikomori behaviors, leading to a deepening disengagement from the real world. Therefore, it becomes vital for individuals and their support networks to strike a balance between utilizing technology as a tool for growth and ensuring it does not hinder the process of overcoming social isolation.

Moreover, the risk of cyberbullying and online harassment cannot be ignored. Those experiencing hikikomori might be particularly vulnerable to these harmful behaviors. The anonymity of the internet can provide an environment where individuals feel emboldened to engage in negative and hurtful actions without immediate, real-life consequences. As such, it is paramount to educate individuals with hikikomori tendencies on online safety, promoting awareness, and establishing strategies to prevent or cope with cyberbullying incidents.

Promoting a Healthy Online Presence:

Recognizing the importance of technology in the lives of individuals with hikikomori tendencies, it becomes essential to outline strategies for fostering a healthy online presence. The key lies in striking a balance between online and offline interactions. Encouraging individuals to gradually increase their engagement with the physical world, while still maintaining connections online, can serve as a stepping stone towards recovery.

Setting clear boundaries and time limits for technology

usage is another crucial aspect of promoting a healthy online presence. By establishing structured routines, individuals can avoid slipping into prolonged periods of isolation and ensure that their online activities do not overshadow real-life responsibilities.

Additionally, it is imperative to emphasize the significance of genuine human connections. While the virtual world can offer comfort and understanding, it is essential to encourage individuals to seek and nurture relationships in the physical world. By fostering real-life connections, individuals can develop interpersonal skills, build resilience, and gradually reintegrate into society.

CONCLUSION:

As we examine the influence of technology and social media on hikikomori behavior, we begin to appreciate the complex interplay between the virtual and physical worlds. While technology can provide both solace and connections, it carries inherent risks that demand vigilance and proactive measures. In the second half of this chapter, we will explore in further depth the challenges faced by individuals navigating the digital landscape and strategies for overcoming them. We will delve into the potential benefits and pitfalls of technology-based interventions and shed light on the multifaceted nature of hikikomori experiences in the age of connectivity.

Stay tuned for the exciting continuation of this exploration.The Dark Side of the Internet: The Dangers and Challenges of Online Spaces

While technology and social media offer individuals with hikikomori tendencies an escape from the pressures of face-to-face interactions, there are inherent risks associated with excessive use of online platforms. In this second half of the chapter, we will delve deeper into the potential pitfalls and challenges faced by individuals navigating the digital landscape.

One significant concern is the phenomenon of online echo chambers. Users often find themselves surrounded by likeminded individuals on social media, participating in communities that reinforce their own beliefs and opinions. While this sense of validation can provide comfort, it can also hinder growth and prevent exposure to diverse perspectives. Without exposure to alternative viewpoints, individuals might develop distorted views of reality, leading to biases and further isolation. It becomes crucial, therefore, to encourage individuals to seek out a broad range of sources for information, fostering critical thinking and a more comprehensive understanding of the world.

Furthermore, the online world can sometimes fuel a

distorted sense of identity and self-worth. Social media platforms, in particular, tend to promote curated versions of ourselves, emphasizing external validation through likes, comments, and followers. For individuals with hikikomori tendencies, this pressure to conform to societal standards can be overwhelming and exacerbate feelings of inadequacy. It is important to help these individuals recognize that their self-worth should not be solely dependent on online interactions and that their true value lies in their unique qualities and abilities. Educating individuals about the artificial nature of online personas and the importance of embracing their authentic selves can empower them to develop genuine self-confidence and build resilience.

In addition to these challenges, the internet poses risks such as online scams, predatory behavior, and exposure to inappropriate content. Individuals experiencing hikikomori may already be vulnerable, making them attractive targets for these dangers. By promoting digital literacy and online safety, individuals can become equipped with the knowledge and skills to navigate the internet responsibly. This includes understanding the importance of strong passwords, being cautious with personal information, and recognizing warning signs of potential scams or malicious intent. Ensuring that individuals are aware of the risks without instilling fear can empower them to engage with online spaces safely and confidently.

Moving beyond the risks, technology can also provide opportunities for growth, development, and overcoming social isolation. With proper guidance and support, individuals can harness the power of technology and social media to engage in creative outlets, learn new skills, and contribute positively to virtual communities. Online platforms dedicated to mental health, personal growth, or hobbies can provide individuals with hikikomori the opportunity to connect with others who share their interests. By participating in these communities, individuals can gradually build their social skills, establish genuine connections, and develop a sense of belonging.

However, it is crucial to strike a balance between the

digital and physical worlds. An excessive reliance on technology for social interaction can impede the journey towards recovery, perpetuating the cycle of isolation. Encouraging individuals to gradually increase their engagement with the physical world is an important aspect of fostering growth and integration. This could involve setting goals for offline activities, such as attending social events, engaging in hobbies outside the home, or seeking professional help through therapy or support groups. By setting achievable goals and providing continuous support, individuals can work towards reestablishing their place in society while still maintaining the benefits of online connections.

Moreover, it is essential to educate individuals about the importance of managing their online presence mindfully. By being selective about the virtual spaces they engage with, individuals can create an online environment that aligns with their values, interests, and personal growth. Developing a healthy online presence includes actively curating one's social media feeds, engaging in positive and constructive discussions, and using social media platforms and technology as tools for personal development rather than sources of escapism.

As we conclude this chapter, it is evident that the role of technology and social media in hikikomori behavior is nuanced and multifaceted. While there are risks and challenges, there are also great opportunities for growth and connection. By proactively addressing these challenges and supporting individuals in their journey towards recovery, we can help them cultivate a healthy relationship with technology and social media.

By fostering digital literacy, promoting critical thinking, and encouraging a balanced usage of online and offline interactions, we pave the way for individuals to overcome social isolation and reintegrate into society with confidence and resilience.

In the next part of this book, we will explore different therapies and interventions that are being used to support individuals with hikikomori tendencies. We will analyze both traditional and technology-based approaches, highlighting their potential benefits in assisting individuals on their path to recovery. Stay tuned for the exciting continuation of this exploration into understanding and overcoming social isolation.

CHAPTER 19: MINDFULNESS AND SELF-CARE PRACTICES

In our modern, interconnected world, the issue of social isolation has become increasingly prevalent. One manifestation of this is a condition known as hikikomori, a term originating from Japan that refers to individuals who choose to isolate themselves from society. These individuals often experience intense feelings of anxiety, depression, and stress, which can have a profound impact on their overall well-being. However, there is hope in the form of mindfulness and self-care practices.

Understanding Hikikomori

To effectively address the challenges faced by individuals experiencing hikikomori, it is important to first gain a deeper understanding of this phenomenon. Hikikomori is not merely a personal choice, but a complex issue influenced by various factors such as societal pressures, cultural expectations, and individual psychosocial dynamics. While the causes may differ from person to person, the consequences are undeniably significant. Understanding the underlying emotional turmoil these individuals face is crucial in formulating effective techniques to reduce stress and improve their overall well-being.

The Power of Mindfulness

Mindfulness, rooted in ancient Buddhist traditions, has gained recognition as a valuable tool to promote mental and emotional well-being. At its core, mindfulness focuses on cultivating awareness and acceptance of the present moment. By engaging in mindfulness practices, individuals experiencing hikikomori can develop a greater sense of self-awareness and gain insights into their thoughts, emotions, and behaviors.

Practicing mindfulness encourages individuals to observe their thoughts and feelings without judgment. This non-reactive stance allows for a fresh perspective, fostering self-compassion and reducing self-criticism. It empowers individuals to acknowledge their emotions and experiences, creating a pathway towards healing and growth. For those trapped in the cycle of social isolation, mindfulness offers a sanctuary to reconnect with themselves and the world around them.

Implementing Mindfulness Techniques

It is essential to introduce practical mindfulness techniques that individuals experiencing hikikomori can incorporate into their daily lives. One such technique is focused breathing. By devoting attention to the sensation of each breath, individuals can anchor themselves in the present moment and momentarily detach from spiraling thoughts and worries. Gradually, this practice allows for a calmer state of mind and an increased ability to handle stressors effectively.

Mindful body awareness is another valuable practice. Encouraging individuals to pay attention to the physical sensations within their bodies enables them to recognize areas of tension, stress, or discomfort. By directing mindful awareness towards these sensations, they can work towards releasing tension, promoting relaxation, and fostering a sense of overall well-being.

Additionally, engaging in mindful activities such as mindful walking or mindful eating can offer a meditative experience. By fully immersing themselves in these activities, individuals can reconnect with their senses and the present moment while cultivating a deeper appreciation for even the simplest of experiences.

Furthermore, integrating guided mindfulness meditations into their routines can assist in managing emotions and promoting emotional resilience. These guided meditations provide individuals with a structured practice that helps them navigate their inner landscapes, recognize negative thought patterns, and foster self-compassion.

The Importance of Self-Care

Alongside mindfulness practices, self-care plays a vital role in the journey towards overcoming social isolation. Self-care encompasses various activities that promote physical, mental, and emotional well-being. It involves prioritizing one's needs, practicing healthy habits, and engaging in activities that bring joy and fulfillment.

For individuals experiencing hikikomori, incorporating self-care practices can prove challenging, given the barriers posed by their isolation. However, it is essential to provide them with accessible and adaptable self-care strategies that empower them to take control of their well-being.

A few self-care practices that can be introduced include ensuring regular physical activity, nourishing the body with a balanced diet, and maintaining a proper sleep routine. Engaging in creative outlets such as painting, writing, or playing a musical instrument can serve as powerful avenues for self-expression and emotional release. Exploring hobbies, engaging in nature, and connecting with supportive online communities can also contribute significantly to one's overall well-being.

Conclusion:

Mindfulness and self-care techniques hold immense potential in supporting individuals experiencing hikikomori on their path towards emotional healing and improved well-being. Through the cultivation of mindfulness, individuals can develop greater self-awareness and self-compassion, enabling them to navigate their emotions more effectively. When coupled with self-care practices, these techniques create a strong foundation for individuals to break free from the chains of social isolation and embrace a life filled with connection, growth, and fulfillment. Part two of this chapter will explore advanced mindfulness practices and additional self-care strategies, delving deeper into the journey of overcoming social isolation. Stay tuned for the next half of this chapter, where we will dive further into the transformative power of mindfulness and self-care practices.Mindfulness and self-care practices offer profound benefits to individuals experiencing hikikomori, empowering them on their journey towards emotional healing and improved well-being. In the first half of this chapter, we explored the power of mindfulness and practical techniques such as focused breathing, mindful body awareness, and engaging in mindful activities. We also emphasized the importance of self-care, encompassing activities that promote physical, mental, and emotional well-being. Now, let us delve deeper into advanced mindfulness practices and additional self-care strategies that can further support individuals in overcoming social isolation.

Advanced Mindfulness Practices

While basic mindfulness techniques can already be transformative, individuals experiencing hikikomori can benefit from advancing their mindfulness practice. One effective technique is loving-kindness meditation. This practice involves cultivating feelings of love, compassion, and kindness towards oneself and others. By internally repeating phrases such as "May I be happy, may I be peaceful, may I be safe," individuals can cultivate a sense of self-compassion and extend their well-wishes towards others. This practice helps break down feelings of isolation and fosters a sense of connection and interdependence with the world.

Another advanced mindfulness practice is open awareness meditation. In this practice, individuals focus on expanding their awareness to include all sensory experiences, thoughts, and emotions without judgment or attachment. By observing and accepting their inner and outer experiences without trying to control or change them, individuals can develop a deeper understanding of themselves and their interconnectedness with the world around them.

Additional Self-Care Strategies

In addition to the previously mentioned self-care practices, there are several other strategies that individuals experiencing hikikomori can adopt to enhance their well-being.

a) Setting Boundaries: Establishing boundaries is crucial for maintaining mental and emotional health. Encourage individuals to learn to say "no" when necessary, prioritize their needs, and communicate their limits effectively to others. By setting boundaries, they can protect their energy and create a safe and supportive environment for their growth.

b) Practicing Gratitude: Cultivating gratitude can have a significant positive impact on one's overall well-being. Encourage individuals to keep a gratitude journal, where they write down three things they are grateful for each day. This practice helps shift their focus towards the positive aspects of their lives, enhancing their resilience and ability to find joy even in challenging circumstances.

c) Seeking Social Support: While hikikomori individuals may struggle with social interactions, it is essential to encourage them to seek supportive relationships. This can be done through online communities, forums, or therapeutic support groups specifically designed for individuals facing similar challenges. Engaging in conversations with like-minded individuals who understand their experiences can provide a sense of validation, connection, and encouragement.

d) Establishing a Routine: Creating a daily routine can provide structure and stability, which are essential for individuals experiencing hikikomori. Encourage them to establish a balanced schedule that includes regular sleep patterns, consistent meal times, exercise, and dedicated time for self-care and mindfulness practices. A well-structured routine can provide a sense of purpose and stability, improving overall well-being.

e) Seeking Professional Help: While self-care practices and mindfulness techniques can be transformative, it is crucial to acknowledge that each individual's journey is unique. In some cases, seeking professional help from therapists, counselors, or psychologists can provide additional guidance and support throughout the healing process. Professional assistance can help individuals address underlying traumas, develop coping mechanisms, and explore new ways of establishing connections.

Conclusion

Mindfulness and self-care practices offer individuals experiencing hikikomori the tools they need to overcome the challenges of social isolation and improve their overall well-being. By advancing their mindfulness practice through techniques like loving-kindness meditation and open awareness meditation, individuals can deepen their self-awareness and cultivate a stronger sense of connectivity with the world around them. Additionally, implementing self-care strategies such as setting boundaries, practicing gratitude, seeking social support, establishing routines, and seeking professional help can further empower individuals in their journey towards healing.

Remember, each step individuals take towards mindfulness and self-care is a testament to their resilience and commitment to their own well-being. By incorporating these practices into their lives, individuals experiencing hikikomori can create a positive impact and pave the way for a future filled with connection, growth, and fulfillment.

CHAPTER 17: REFLECTION AND
MOVING FORWARD

In our journey to understand and overcome social isolation, we have delved deep into the world of Hikikomori, exploring its causes, consequences, and potential solutions. Throughout this book, we have examined the factors leading to social withdrawal, the experiences of individuals affected by Hikikomori, and the impact on families and society as a whole. Now, it is time to reflect on the key concepts we have discussed and outline the steps for progress in overcoming this issue.

Reflection is an essential process in any transformative journey. It allows us to gain insights, learn from our experiences, and make positive changes moving forward. Throughout our exploration of Hikikomori, we have unraveled the intricate web of factors contributing to social isolation. We have recognized that a combination of societal pressure, academic stress, mental health challenges, and cultural factors can lead individuals to withdraw from society as a coping mechanism.

Moreover, we have acknowledged that social media, although intended to connect people, can inadvertently exacerbate the problem. The constant comparison to others' seemingly perfect lives and the fear of judgment can deepen feelings of isolation and inadequacy. Understanding these underlying causes is crucial in developing effective strategies to combat Hikikomori and promote social inclusivity.

Summarizing the key concepts discussed so far, we have come to realize that Hikikomori is not solely an individual issue. Instead, it reflects broader societal problems that need to be addressed collaboratively. It is essential to create an empathetic and compassionate environment where individuals struggling with Hikikomori do not feel isolated or judged. Families, educational institutions, medical professionals, and society as a whole must work together to break the cycle of social withdrawal.

To move forward in combating Hikikomori, we must focus on several key steps. First and foremost, awareness and education are paramount. By increasing understanding about the challenges faced by individuals experiencing social isolation, we can dispel common misconceptions and promote empathy. Educational campaigns at schools, workplaces, and within communities can help reduce stigma and create an environment of support.

Secondly, early intervention is crucial in tackling Hikikomori. Identifying signs of withdrawal in individuals and addressing their concerns promptly can prevent the long-term consequences of isolation. Schools and educational institutions should implement comprehensive mental health programs that provide counseling, support, and resources to students who may be at risk.

Furthermore, fostering social inclusivity and acceptance is essential. Society must work towards creating an environment that celebrates diversity and embraces individuals as they are, without judgment or prejudice. Promoting social integration and offering inclusive opportunities for involvement, such as community programs and activities, can help individuals affected by Hikikomori reconnect with society.

Lastly, collaboration between different stakeholders is key to achieving lasting change. Governments, healthcare providers, educators, families, and individuals themselves must join forces to design and implement effective policies, interventions, and support networks. This multidimensional approach will ensure a comprehensive response to Hikikomori and instigate a positive transformation in society's perception and treatment of social isolation.

In conclusion, our first half of Chapter 20 has provided an overview of the key concepts discussed throughout this book. We have reflected on the causes and consequences of Hikikomori and emphasized the importance of collaboration, awareness, early intervention, and social inclusivity in combatting this issue. By applying these principles, we can pave the way for a more inclusive and supportive society. However, our journey is not complete. The second half of this chapter will further delve into practical strategies and inspiring stories of individuals who have overcome social isolation.

Stay tuned for the second part, which will unveil the next steps towards understanding and overcoming Hikikomori.In the second half of this chapter, we will delve deeper into practical strategies and inspiring stories of individuals who have overcome social isolation, focusing on their journey towards understanding and overcoming Hikikomori. By sharing these stories, we hope to provide hope and guidance for those currently experiencing social withdrawal and inspire collective action in combating this issue.

One of the key strategies in addressing Hikikomori is empowering individuals to take the first steps towards reconnecting with society. It can be a challenging process, especially for those who have experienced long periods of isolation and anxiety. However, exploring personal interests and passions can serve as a starting point for rebuilding social connections. Engaging in hobbies, sports, art, or volunteer work can provide a sense of purpose, boost self-esteem, and create opportunities for meeting like-minded individuals.

We must also recognize the significant role that families play in supporting individuals affected by Hikikomori. Family members often experience their own feelings of confusion, guilt, and helplessness. To overcome these challenges, it is essential for families to seek professional guidance, such as therapy or support groups, where they can learn effective communication strategies, coping mechanisms, and how to set healthy boundaries.

By fostering a nurturing and understanding home environment, families can become a stronghold of support for their loved ones, promoting their reintegration into society.

Alongside individuals and families, educational institutions also have a crucial role in combating Hikikomori.

Schools should prioritize mental health education and implement comprehensive support programs that include regular mental health check-ups, counseling services, and anti-bullying initiatives. By addressing these issues at an early stage, schools can provide a safety net for students facing social isolation, preventing long-term consequences.

Moreover, creating a supportive and inclusive environment within educational institutions is paramount. By fostering a culture of acceptance, empathy, and understanding, students will feel more comfortable seeking help and sharing their experiences. Implementing peer support programs, organizing student-led initiatives, and promoting open dialogue about mental health are effective ways to encourage social inclusivity within schools.

Society as a whole must also play a proactive role in combating Hikikomori. Governments, in collaboration with healthcare providers, need to allocate resources and funding to improve mental health services, particularly those targeting social withdrawal. By increasing access to affordable and quality mental health care, individuals affected by Hikikomori can receive the support they need to reintegrate into society successfully.

Promoting public awareness and understanding is another crucial aspect of combating social isolation. Media outlets, social influencers, and public figures should responsibly use their platforms to shed light on the realities of Hikikomori, debunk misconceptions, and promote empathy and understanding towards those experiencing social withdrawal. Through educational campaigns, documentaries, and public forums, the broader community can gain a deeper appreciation for the challenges faced by individuals affected by Hikikomori, reducing stigma and fostering a compassionate society.

Lastly, the importance of maintaining a multidimensional approach in tackling Hikikomori cannot be emphasized enough. Collaboration between various stakeholders, including individuals, families, educators, healthcare providers, and policymakers, is essential for developing holistic solutions. By sharing resources, knowledge, and experiences, these stakeholders can work together to design and implement effective policies, interventions, and support networks that address the diverse needs of those experiencing social isolation.

In conclusion, we already have explored several practical strategies and went through inspiring stories of individuals who have overcome social isolation, signaling hope and possibilities for change.

By empowering individuals, supporting families, reforming educational systems, and promoting societal awareness, we can continue the momentum in combating Hikikomori and nurturing a more inclusive and compassionate society. Let us embark on this journey together, with the shared commitment to understanding and overcoming social isolation.

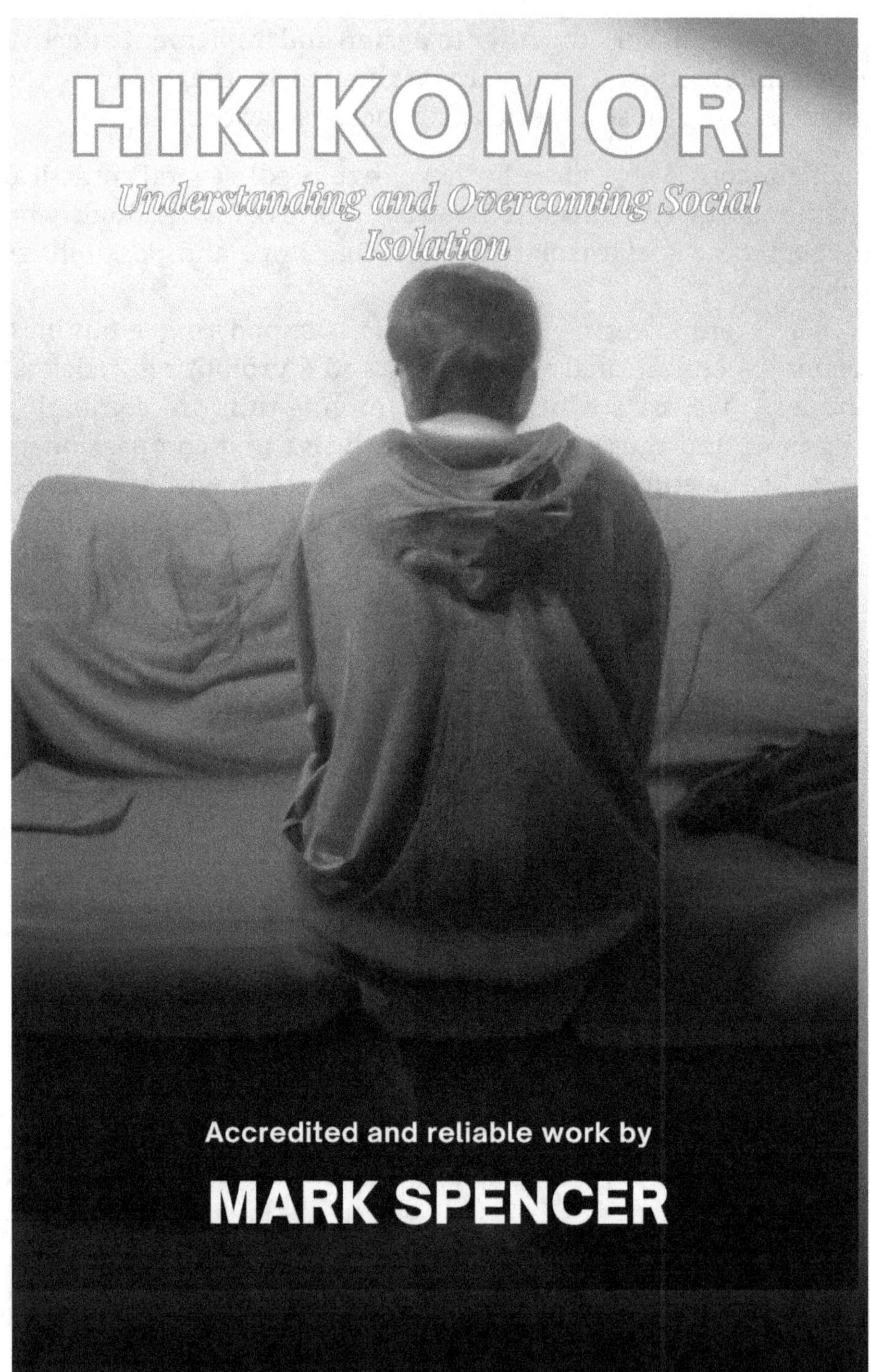
HIKIKOMORI
Understanding and Overcoming Social Isolation
Accredited and reliable work by
MARK SPENCER

ABOUT THE AUTHOR

Dr. Mark Spencer, a retired child psychologist with a distinguished career dedicated to understanding and treating psychological disorders in children and adolescents, brings a wealth of knowledge to the topic of Hikikomori. His extensive experience, grounded in psychology and bolstered by his direct work with affected individuals, offers a unique perspective on the causes, manifestations, and interventions for Hikikomori. Dr. Spencer's transition from active practice to writing allows him to share his insights and strategies for addressing this complex issue, aiming to enlighten both professionals and families on effective approaches to support those experiencing extreme social withdrawal.

www.ingramcontent.com/pod-product-compliance
Lightning Source LLC
Chambersburg PA
CBHW070806260726
48660CB00005B/1737